Cargo Crime

Security and Theft Prevention

Cargo Crime

Security and Theft Prevention

J.J. Coughlin

CRC Press
Taylor & Francis Group
Boca Raton   London   New York

CRC Press is an imprint of the
Taylor & Francis Group, an **informa** business

CRC Press
Taylor & Francis Group
6000 Broken Sound Parkway NW, Suite 300
Boca Raton, FL 33487-2742

© 2013 by Taylor & Francis Group, LLC
CRC Press is an imprint of Taylor & Francis Group, an Informa business

No claim to original U.S. Government works

Printed in the United States of America on acid-free paper
Version Date: 20120808

International Standard Book Number: 978-1-4665-1245-0 (Hardback)

Library of Congress Cataloging-in-Publication Data

Coughlin, John J.
  Cargo crime : security and theft prevention / John J. Coughlin.
    p. cm.
  Includes bibliographical references and index.
  ISBN 978-1-4665-1245-0 (hardcover : alk. paper)
    1. Cargo theft--United States--Prevention. 2. Freight and freightage--Security measures--United States. 3. Freight and freightage--Law and legislation--United States.
  I. Title.

  HV6658.C685 2013
  388′.0440684--dc23   2012029901

Visit the Taylor & Francis Web site at
http://www.taylorandfrancis.com

and the CRC Press Web site at
http://www.crcpress.com

Contents

SECTION III   USING BEST PRACTICES

Foreword

Professionals involved in supply chain security will discover that *Cargo Crime: Security and Theft Prevention* by J.J. Coughlin is both an indispensable overview of current cargo trends and a viable desktop reference for field practitioners whose job it is to establish security plans and predictive security operations in the transportation and logistics fields.

This book was based on the premise that the wealth of experience in law enforcement, cargo theft investigation, and cargo theft intelligence analysis accumulated by the author as director of the Supply Chain Information Sharing and Analysis Center has given him an insight and understanding of the criminal elements involved in these crimes that he wanted to share with investigators and transportation security practitioners. He achieved his goal and has produced a text that will pass on to those who peruse it the benefit of his years of practical experience in the specialty area of cargo crime.

The text is organized into a scenario that will enable the novice or the grizzled veteran to proceed from Chapter 1, "Cargo Crime: Definition and Trends," to observing charts and information that will answer the four basic questions (what, where, when, and how) of crime. By the time the reader proceeds through Chapter 3, "Perpetrators of Cargo Crime," he or she will be able to answer the fifth and final crime question: who.

Collectively, the chapters of this book represent a source and definitive guide for transportation security managers and law enforcement personnel. It has been designed to reveal the experiences of the author in a practical, useful, and progressive manner. The research is empirical and the results compiled into this text will be relevant for many years.

After answering the basic crime questions, the book takes you through the responses of industries to build an information-sharing and communication system through regional security councils that focus on highlighting risks and threats via a shared BOLO/Alert program and providing a networking system with law enforcement to respond to crimes. The text also provides information on products and solutions designed to prevent cargo crime and a highly useful glossary of transportation security and freight terms along with abbreviations as an important addendum to the information in the chapters.

As a transportation attorney for more than 27 years, I consider this book a must read for any transportation professional. J.J. Coughlin has tackled a very complicated subject. He presents the material in an easy-to-understand review along with solutions that are timeless.

Steven E. Lewis
Lewis & Backhaus, P.C.
Dallas, Texas

Preface

The purpose of *Cargo Crime: Security and Theft Prevention* is to provide practical conventional current information for transportation and logistics industry and law enforcement units and officers responsible for the security of supply chains and the investigation of those who prey upon them.

This text is based on the author's personal experiences as a law enforcement detective and supervisor and as a regional security manager for a large multimode transportation and logistics company. This experience, along with many years of serving as the director of the Supply Chain Information Sharing and Analysis Center (SC-ISAC)—an organization that collects and analyzes cargo crime data and shares information with transportation security experts—provides a thorough overview of illicit activities impacting supply chains.

Analyzing cargo crime trends and patterns and using the information derived to identify methods of operation of organized and opportunistic criminals who target supply chains extremely helpful for determining risks and threats. The ability to apply that information based on real world experience and industry associations makes the information that much more usable. If you look at the reference material for this book, most of it was originally prepared by the author in his role as chairman of the Southwest Transportation Security Council in collaboration with many council members who are subject matter experts in specific areas.

In order to be successful, an industry security practitioner must have an eye for detail while understanding the risks and complexities of cargo operations so that the correct security and recovery plan applied to a situation will be both effective and cost-efficient.

One thing is certain: cargo security is much trickier than just throwing guards, technology, and money at the problem. Applying the right resource for the involved mode and issue takes a true understanding of all of the variables. This book attempts to identify and discuss those variables and make each practitioner cognizant of the options available. This book will cover the current trends, cargo criminal operational methods, and best practices and solutions for each circumstance. Protection of cargo is not simple; it requires the ability to use all the information presented. No single solution fits all situations, as shown in this book.

The investigation of cargo crime is hindered by a lack of true federal response. Adequate law enforcement assistance, particularly aiding recovery, is an issue industry has taken to heart and pursued via industry councils, information sharing, and building police networking in areas where crimes and criminals are prevalent. This book speaks to those councils, their activities, and their continuing push forward despite the lack of cargo theft statutes in many states and the deficiency of law enforcement cargo theft task forces in many jurisdictions where they are sorely needed.

This book speaks to law enforcement training provided by the industry and covers company operations and documentation. It deals with the subject of commercial vehicle interdiction in a way I have not seen in other cargo-related writings. Many volumes have been written on this subject, frequently in manual format, and not based on real experience from investigation and security management in the transportation security field. It has been my intention to present a factual down-to-earth cargo theft handbook based on true experience and ongoing involvement in the field. This book stresses the basics of cargo crime and provides the reader with patterns and trends upon which to build a solid foundation for construction of a company security and recovery plan along with information to assist law enforcement with investigations. I recommend that the reader absorb the information related in the text and realize that it includes strategically placed repetition because certain known principles can never be stressed enough.

I truly hope this book will be an informative, enjoyable, and interesting read for those who have interest in this complicated and amazingly underreported criminal activity.

Acknowledgments

I want to personally thank and acknowledge the many people, agencies, associations, and councils that contributed to *Cargo Crime: Security and Theft Prevention*. Their professional expertise, suggestions, photographs, and information encouraged me to complete this text. Since I am not a professional author, I needed all the help I could get. I am listing these persons in alphabetical order and hope I have not inadvertently omitted anyone.

Thanks to Mary Aftanas, NICB; Jerry Allen, NICB; Jennifer Bennett, Polo Ralph Lauren; Charles Bergeron, FedEx; Wayne Browning, Texas Association of Vehicle Theft Investigators; Hans Bryson, Dallas Police Department, Retired; Stephen Burau, Ryder Logistics; Nolan Burns, FedEx Freight; Sgt. Steve Covey, Mid-West Cargo Task Force; Pat Clancy, LoJack Law Enforcement; Murry Cohen, CNF, Retired; Scott Cornell, Travelers Insurance SIU; Brian Coughlin, Dallas County District Attorney's Office; Karen Coughlin, Hilton Bella Harbor; Phil Crepeau, LoJack Law Enforcement; Eric De La Barre, Southeast Transportation Security Council; Sheriff Ed Dean, Marion County (Florida) and National Cargo Theft Task Force; Millie DeAnda, NTCC; Shawn Driscoll, Swift Transportation; Kurt Duesterdick, Eastern Regional Cargo Theft Association; Nick Economu, Schneider National; Randy Ferguson, Ferguson Investigations; Chuck Forsaith, Pharmaceutical Cargo Security Coalition; Robert Furtado, LoJack Supply Chain Integrity; Rob Gammon, HP Global Security; Laura Hains, ASIS Supply Chain

Security Council; Ivy Haley, Fort Worth Police Department;
Jeff Hall, PI Transit Risk Management; Merri Hawkins,
California Highway Patrol, Cargo Theft Interdiction Program;
Kevin Heath, CNet Technologies; John Heil, Conway Freight;
Patrick Hientz, Texas Department of Public Safety; Stacy
Hohenberger, NICB; Sgt. Mike Hoyt, Dallas Police Department
UCR; Kevin Johnson, Panalpina NA; Mike Johnston, DSC
Security; Steve Keller, Menlo Logistics, Retired; Michelle
Lanham, Texas Auto Burglary Theft Prevention Authority;
Keith Lewis, CargoNet; Steve E. Lewis, Lewis & Backhaus,
P.C. and SWTSC; Fred Lohmann, NICB; Rick Martin, Knight
Transportation, ATA, and S&LP; Patti Martinez, Floodlight Press;
Sgt. Kevin Mathias, ISP Mid-West Cargo Task Force; Ed Matis,
Dallas Police Department; Sheri McKinney, ATS; Kevin Mazza,
HP Global Security and Mid-West Cargo Task Force; Willie
Morales, Miami Dade Police Department; Jim Morgan, Ryder
Logistics; Charles Morton, Panalpina NA; John Murphy, Texas
Department of Public Safety; Jaime Olivarez, Yellow Freight;
Ray Rios, SAIA Freight; Vance Root, US Risk; Tom Sheets, CNF,
Retired; Alan Spear, Transported Asset Protection Association;
Michelle Standifer, A&O Photography; Geoff Stefany, ODFL;
Lt. Randy Stewart, Texas Department of Public Safety; John
Tabor, National Retail Systems; April Tiger, SC-ISAC; Carlos
Velez, ASIS Supply Chain Security Council; Mark Walicki, DEA,
Retired; David Wallace, Dallas Police Department, Retired; Tina
Weatherford, Dr. Pepper; Ted Wlazkowski, LoJack Supply Chain
Integrity; John Yakstas, Ryder Logistics; and Mark Zavala, Los
Angeles Police Department.

Special thanks are extended to my wife Lynette, son Kyle,
and extended family members for their support and encour-
agement during the writing process.

Each person listed above contributed in some way directly
or indirectly, through participation in the real-life incidents
discussed in the book or through information shared with the
Southwest Transportation Security Council (SWTSC).

About the Author

John Joseph (J.J.) Coughlin is currently vice president of law enforcement services for LoJack Supply Chain Integrity (SCI). He is responsible for developing, implementing, and overseeing security processes, procedures, and investigations for SCI members. J.J. also works closely with law enforcement officers in deployment of LoJack In-Transit Service to support covert surveil-
lance, dispatch, and recovery operations and investigations. He also serves as the director of the Supply Chain Information Sharing and Analysis Center (SC-ISAC) and supervises the collection, analysis, and dissemination of cargo theft and crime data.

J.J. serves as the chairman of the Southwest Transportation Security Council, which he founded to facilitate the sharing of information and networking with law enforcement and private industry. He has been a driving force behind the expansion of regional security councils and promoting information sharing by regional councils, law enforcement, and private industry. He is an active member of the Western States Cargo Theft Association, Southeast Transportation Security Council, Virginia–Carolinas Cargo Security Council, American Society for Industrial Security (ASIS) Supply Chain Security Committee, International Associations of Chiefs of Police, International Association of Auto Theft Investigators, Advisory Committee of the National Cargo Theft Task Force, National Council of Information Sharing and Analysis Centers (ISACs), and the Trans-Border International Police Association. J.J. also conducts security consulting duties for Trans-Secure Compliance and Solutions.

Before joining LoJack, SCI, J.J. spent 10 years in the transportation industry as a regional security manager for CNF/Conway, a national transportation and logistics company. Prior to joining CNF/Conway, he spent 22 years with the Dallas Police Department and was assigned for 17 of those years as a detective or supervisor in the areas of areas assault, homicide, intelligence, and public integrity. J.J. has also instructed classes in interview and interrogation techniques and supply chain and cargo transportation related subjects.

OVERVIEW OF CARGO CRIME

Chapter 1

Cargo Crime: Definition and Trends

Introduction

Cargo theft. When you hear or see those words, you may imagine piracy on the high seas, stagecoach and train robberies in the old west, or some other long-ago image of a romantic criminal element dramatically represented by the entertainment media as the good old days. Cargo theft has been portrayed as acceptable behavior. Robin Hood and his merry men would inflict brutality on the king's men in the process of stealing the kingdom's goods and gold to share with the less fortunate. Stories about the likes of Butch Cassidy and the Sundance Kid and their Hole-in-the-Wall Gang along with Jesse and Frank James and the Younger Brothers also entertained us. Who can forget Detective Axel Foley in *Beverly Hills Cop* as he rode in the back of a hijacked trailer containing a load of stolen cigarettes?

Cargo theft has been a part of American history ever since people started moving products by conveyances—whether horse, wagon train, or Pony Express. As society and transportation and logistics methods evolved, cargo criminals and their methods progressed to meet the industrial changes but the intent to deprive an owner of rightful property remains the same.

Cargo crime has always been lucrative for the criminal element but probably never more so than today. Classification as a property crime allows cargo theft to present low risks and yield high rewards. Risk is low because the justice system imposes small penalties on property crimes while stolen products bring high-dollar rewards to perpetrators. Even opportunistic thieves who will take just about anything can turn stolen goods for ten cents on the dollar in a short time. A $20,000 load will produce good pay for a short day's work. The organized thieves continue to challenge much more expensive loads but when caught usually net light sentences.

In this book, we are going to look at cargo theft in the United States in the 21st century. Cargo theft is a global problem, but that is another book for another time. We are going to focus on domestic theft issues and related criminal methods. It is important to understand these issues, the risks and developments, so that persons and companies involved in the US supply chain can make the assessments of their individual risks based on their operations and the commodities they ship, manufacture, carry, store, handle, or insure.

It is important to understand which commodities present the highest risks, how those commodities are targeted, where the thefts occur, how the criminals operate, and why they choose the crime of cargo theft. All these points are very important to the analysis of current trends and patterns. We will look at charts from the Supply Chain Information Sharing and Analysis Center (SC-ISAC) that will answer several of the questions and then look at criminal methods of operation to resolve the who and why questions.

But before we look at the charts and analyze the loss information, it is important to examine the impact of cargo theft. The results are very far reaching and involve far more than the direct losses shown in statistics and charts. When a cargo theft occurs, whether during transit or from a warehouse or terminal, the missing product and equipment represent direct losses from a criminal act. The total losses from such offenses average around $200,000.00 *per theft*. So what is the indirect loss? The indirect loss will include the cost of replacing the missing shipment by remanufacturing the lost inventory. It also includes losses incurred because the consignee does not receive the product it needs for sale or use. The carrier's loss arises from not having access to missing equipment. Another indirect loss is the insurance cost to cover the cargo and equipment. When you add all of the indirect factors, you see that the cost of one criminal act produces huge consequences.

We will also look at the current law enforcement response to cargo crime and how it is dealt with in various areas of the country. Based on this law enforcement response, we will see how the transportation and logistics industry has stepped up to promote cargo crime awareness, share information, educate and network with law enforcement, and seek preventative alternatives to overcome the current criminal methods of cargo crime perpetrators. It is important to impress on the industry that the protection of its operations is not provided by any government agency. The National Strategy for Global Supply Chain Security is no more a company security plan than a call to 911 is a comprehensive recovery plan.

Solutions and industry best practices applying to the current threats and known criminal methods will be provided and discussed in an effort to give industry operators a checklist to aid security through various parts of the supply chain including physical, in-transit, personnel, and procedural guidelines.

When I was tasked to write this book, I did not want it to be a manual written by someone who studied the issue or was involved in security from a research or academic standpoint. I wanted to bring about awareness of current cargo theft trends and intertwine it with my own experiences from working in the industry, conducting investigations, and observing at the grassroots level. I wanted to take all of the data we currently collect and analyze at the SC-ISAC and put a stamp of reality on it, make sense of what it means from the views of studying cargo crime and having actually lived with it.

I read several other books and saw that they were written from a different perspective—not after doing dirty work in the trenches and building relationships with industry security professionals from whom I continue to learn. As you read this book, I make references to many cases I actually worked. I tried to relay personal experiences and the reality of being a regional security manager tasked with problem solving and investigative responsibility over multiple locations and business units covering a large territory including a foreign country.

Background and Perspective

My first experience with cargo theft came long before I had any real knowledge of the subject. As a young patrol officer in the mid 1970s, I worked a patrol beat covering a government housing project adjacent to a railroad switching yard. We spent quite a bit of time chasing, investigating, and apprehending thieves, both juvenile and adult, who were "shopping" the rail cars for usable goods. We made many arrests and recovered a plethora of railroad client property in private residences in the government housing unit.

I spent quite a bit of time working with the railroad police and assisting them with operations and property issues. This experience was beneficial because I learned quite a bit about the operations of railroads, insurance guidelines on the recovered property, and how the railroad police jurisdiction and rules worked in coordination with the Texas Penal Code and Code of Criminal Procedures. During my time on that beat, we worked on many thefts and burglaries; a railroad police officer shot and killed a thief during an incident on the tracks. The rail yard provided plenty of activity and useful experience in dealing with cargo crime early in my law enforcement career. After leaving that assignment, I spent the next 17 years as a detective or detective supervisor responsible for many types of crimes not related to cargo.

In 1997, after spending almost 22 years with a large municipal police department in Texas, I retired from police work and detective toil to enter the private sector. Leaving the police department was not a sad day; I never really longed to be an officer. When I joined the department, I just needed a job. It is still hard to believe I stayed that long.

I accepted a position with a large, multifaceted transportation and logistics company. I was hired as its southwest regional manager of security responsible for Texas, five other states, and Mexico. This operation included a freight airline, a freight forwarding company, a third party logistics company, a full truckload company, and two less-than-truckload companies (one union and one nonunion). I was tasked with security responsibilities for all the company entities in my assigned territory. My police experience taught me how to investigate, interview, and interrogate, but I soon found that I had very little knowledge about transportation and logistics security operations.

Since I was new to the industry, this assignment seemed overwhelming at first, but it actually turned out to be a great benefit. I had to learn quickly what freight transportation security was all about. The security needs for an industry are as complex as the industry itself. Unless one works across an entire industry, it is difficult to understand the workings of all the moving parts (shippers, carriers, logistic providers, insurers, brokers, vendors) involved in the many ways to move, store, and distribute product; and the coordination required of the participants. Moving a box, a pallet, or a truckload from point A to point B, on its face seems like a simple proposition, but it is far more complicated than it appears. One must first learn the language and acronyms of the industry and master the documentation, transportation modes, and freight movement details. The wide variety of modes and operations involved in a large logistics and transportation enterprise meant a very steep learning curve, but with the assistance of patient operations personnel, I quickly found my way.

So let's take a good look at the cargo theft issues, the industry, and the current law enforcement response to the problem.

Definition of Cargo Theft

Let's start with a definition. Cargo theft can occur by many different criminal activities such as theft, burglary, robbery, and even fraud. I suppose the official or best all-inclusive definition of cargo theft is the one provided by the Federal Bureau of Investigation Uniform Crime Reporting Program's National Incident-Based Reporting System (NIBRS):

> *Cargo theft* is the criminal taking of any cargo including, but not limited to, goods, chattels, money, or baggage that constitutes, in whole or in part, a commercial shipment of freight moving in commerce, from any pipeline system, railroad car, motor truck, or other vehicle, or from any tank or storage facility, station house, platform, or depot, or from any vessel or wharf, or from any aircraft, air terminal, airport, aircraft terminal or air navigation facility, or from any intermodal container, intermodal chassis, trailer, container freight station, warehouse, freight distribution facility, or freight consolidation facility. For purposes of this definition, cargo shall be deemed as moving in commerce at all points between the point of origin and the final destination, regardless of any temporary stop while awaiting trans-shipment or otherwise (USDOJ n.d.).

This definition illustrates one cargo theft problem faced by industry and law enforcement. Crime reporting and classification are much more complex than one would think. Each law enforcement jurisdiction in the United States has a reporting system specific to its operation. Every state has a distinct set of criminal laws and codes not tied to those of other states. The National Crime Information Center (NCIC) stores some crime data, but little or no integration and communication exist among local, county, state, and federal agencies.

When I first came into the transportation industry and started networking with transportation security professionals, the great need was to quantify the cargo crime problem. If you follow this subject, you will have noted estimates of billions of dollars per year lost to cargo crime, but no factual, recordable, or researchable data to back up those numbers have been compiled. Many thought the unified crime report (UCR) code for cargo theft would eventually assist the industry in quantifying losses.

As someone who has worked in both law enforcement and industry, I do not believe the UCR system will be able to provide a true quantification of cargo losses. First, all of the separate agencies would have to use the UCR system and correctly code reported offenses. Complete reporting is almost totally improbable because of individual case facts and the need to distinguish between a cargo crime in the supply chain versus a regular commercial building burglary or armed hijacking. Also, a specific cargo theft statute is needed in each state jurisdiction to allow a match with the federal UCR code. Every industry operates in many different modes under many different contracts, claims, and insurance programs. No industry will report all of its losses to law enforcement simply because so many exceptions are handled through internal and contractual claims processes. Such internal systems hamper true offense counts and reporting.

These real issues prevent the UCR code from providing true quantification of the problem. We will talk about many of these issues later in the book when we discuss the different modes of freight transportation.

Current Data and Data Collection Efforts

Several different entities now collect cargo theft data and much of the information is collected from and shared with many of the same sources. All these groups know that the data they collect does not cover all the cargo crime that occurs, but after years of collection and allowing the databases to mature, a true analysis can be performed to provide industry and law enforcement with current trends and methods of cargo crime activities.

As the director of the Supply Chain Information Sharing and Analysis Center (SC-ISAC), I have been involved in the collection and analysis of such data since 2007. We will look at some of the past data and see what we have been able to collect and learn. I will show you some charts and data that allow us to understand the current threats and risks involved in the transportation and logistics industry.

Let's look back a little before we move forward. The SC-ISAC started collecting cargo theft information from multiple sources in 2006. It took several years for the data to mature, more sources to be found, and data collection to be enhanced. By 2007, enough data existed to start looking for trends and information, but it really wasn't until around 2009 that the data set matured enough to provide a reliable overall picture. Although we identified much information on methods and suspects before data analysis by industry, insurance, and law enforcement, the true picture started to evolve through the records by 2009.

We wanted our analysis to be able to answer the who, what, where, why, and how surrounding cargo crimes. We also wanted to compare the SC-ISAC information to similar reports provided by insurance companies and other industry resources. While we knew that the SC-ISAC did not receive all cargo theft data, neither did the other sources. We were looking for similarities from those sources to assist in the confirmation of our data analysis. As each collector's data matured and underwent a comparison to the SC-ISAC information, the identified trends and information were confirmed and enhanced. The following information and charts will give us vital and vetted information from which to start analyzing the current cargo theft and cargo crime issues.

When we understand how cargo thieves operate, we can take the correct preventative measures to reduce risk. The charts in this chapter will show thefts by state, location type, time factors, and items targeted by both organized and opportunistic thieves and assist us in understanding cargo crime trends and the criminal methods of involved parties. After you "have a handle" on that information as an industry security practitioner, you will be able to put a security plan in place for your operation, with a focus on prevention and the ability to include a fail-safe system for recovery. You will be able to direct the police during recovery efforts because you will understand current cargo criminal methods and be able to predict their actions after a theft. This knowledge will also allow you to successfully devise company security and recovery plans.

Analysis of SC-ISAC Data for 2009–2011

The SC-ISAC recorded 2,264 incidents in 2009, 2010, and 2011. Of those, 611 incidents for 2009, 813 for 2010, and 678 for 2011, totaling 2,102, were categorized as cargo thefts for the three-year period. The remaining 162 incidents were classified as frauds, burglaries, or robberies. The SC-ISAC also issued intelligence reports to assist law enforcement investigations seeking complainants or information on cargo-related incidents. Based on reported incidents, the losses of both cargoes and vehicles for the three-year period totaled $414,960,152 or $197,412 per reported incident. Most incidents involved thefts from full truckload carriers. The SC-ISAC collects and archives types of freight stolen, where it is stolen, state and type of location (crime scene), time stolen, and location of recovery of equipment and/or freight.

At the SC-ISAC, we take great care to make sure that we do not overreport the incidents we receive—which is easily done when taking batch information from law enforcement agencies. While the SC-ISAC does not gather anywhere near the full number of cargo theft incidents, the last thing we want to do is duplicate or count an incident more than once. The center does not amass every single incident nor ever expect to; its goal is to not quantify an issue but to conduct analysis of the information collected to make determinations that can help supply chain operators understand the risks, raise their levels of awareness, and allow them to prepare security and recovery plans based on the knowledge and analyzed information.

As you scour the loss and recovery data, please keep the following points in mind:

1. Dollar amounts are often estimated by the information provider, usually only to include direct loss information; they could possibly change as an investigation progresses.
2. Dollar amounts are typically only provided for the items owned or insured by the information provider and may not represent the total loss sustained.
3. Single-load losses, especially for high-value Items such as pharmaceuticals, can skew the average loss figures.

A review of three years of collected cargo theft data reveals quite a jump in reported numbers in 2010 and then a little step back in 2011. We continue to see the fraudulent pick-up category increase and we want to keep our eyes open to new and effective cargo criminal methods. The SC-ISAC also records locations where the stolen items are recovered. From this data, we can make logical determinations about current and changing criminal methods. By tracking data over the past three years, we have seen a change in the movement of stolen products and evidence of the development of splinter groups in several new and different locations. The methods of targeting products and committing thefts remain consistent, but stolen products are handled differently now in several geographical areas.

Cargo Theft Activity by State

Cargo theft activity has long been thought of as a crime that knows no geographic boundaries as shown by the increasing number of states reporting activities ranging from in-transit thefts to warehouse and carrier facility thefts. For the three-year period from 2009 through 2011, we see more and more states sending in reports and information. Even though data for the top seven to ten states have remained consistent, this is only one of four or five factors from which one can prepare an in-transit security plan.

As we look at the 2011 chart, California has by far reported the most cargo theft activity in North America, holding the top spot the entire year. Texas, New Jersey, Georgia, Illinois, Pennsylvania, and Tennessee have each appeared among the top reporting states for all four quarters. Florida was one of the most active states, listed for three of the four quarters. We believe Florida has much more activity than reported to the SC-ISAC and the charts currently show. Florida would probably be a constant second or third if all the data were obtained. The data the SC-ISAC collected enabled us to conduct the analysis and make good logical determinations about cargo thefts and their impacts.

Figure 1.1 shows the consistency in where the thefts occur. I believe that reporting increases in states where industry and law enforcement work together to share information through industry councils and cargo theft task forces. This public–private partnership activity invites a much more open exchange of information and reporting than is possible in

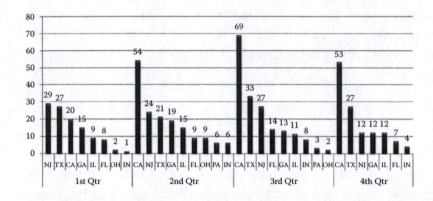

Figure 1.1 The top eight states subject to cargo thefts seldom change; only their order on the charts changes.

states that do not have that advantage. I believe the data sources and information sharing will continue to grow to paint an even better picture of the cargo theft problem, but we already have a pretty clear idea from the data we analyzed. When you break the information down further within the listed states, you find that most theft occurs in highly populated areas (big cities and metropolitan areas) within those states as a result of the routing of interstate freeway networks through major hubs.

In California, most activity occurs in the southern section in and around Los Angeles. In Texas, the focus is on the Dallas and Houston metropolitan areas; Chicago is the main location in Illinois. Tennessee cargo crimes center in Memphis and Nashville and most Florida activity is around Miami. Most people in the cargo industry know that the Atlanta area in Georgia is notorious and cargo theft action freely crosses the state line between Pennsylvania and New Jersey.

I reviewed a recent California Highway Patrol (CHP) Cargo Theft Interdiction Program Report (Hawkins 2011). In an analysis of cargo theft by state, California was cited at the top of the list, followed by Texas, New Jersey, Florida, Illinois, and Georgia. This conclusion is in line with the SC-ISAC

data and information from other sources. When CHP analyzed the cargo crime locations in California, 61% occurred in
the greater Los Angeles area followed by 22% in the Inland
Empire (Riverside and San Bernardino Counties).

Where Thefts Occur

If you were going to steal a cargo rig, where would you go?
Organized theft groups know the correct answer: the first
location where the equipment and cargo are left unattended
and thus present an opportunity to thieves.

Between 2009 and 2011, three cargo theft locations (truck
stops, carrier facilities, parking lots) jostled for the dubious
distinction of the top location for cargo theft activity. In 2009,
truck stops took the top spot while carrier facilities easily
carried 2010. Throughout 2010 the SC-ISAC reported a more
strategic approach by cargo thieves. The 2010 data illustrated
a significant shift from 2009 when truck stops held the top
spot. Figure 1.2 shows that truck stops and parking lots lead
throughout the 2011 data.

The number of incidents where locations are not specified
is substantially higher than in past years, and is due primarily to batch data received from the California Highway Patrol
(CHP) and the New Jersey State Police that required further
analysis. While the SC-ISAC encourages members to provide
the most detailed theft information possible, it is not always
feasible. When looking at this information, the most striking
determination is that the thefts will happen at almost any type
of location where a driver leaves a rig and cargo unattended,
especially if the load contains one of the targeted commodities
identified in cargo theft data.

According to Figure 1.2, truck stop, carrier facilities, and
parking lots are the top three locations. Data for the previous
year are similar. But what you really learn from this graphic
is that a criminal using methods we will discuss later in this

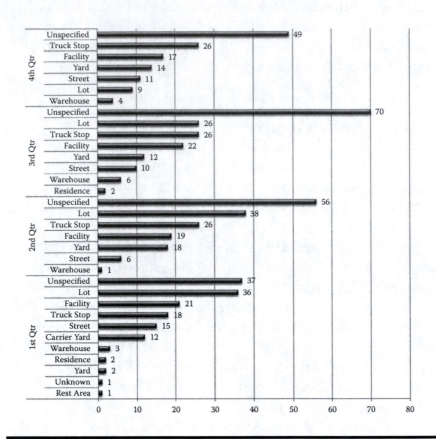

Figure 1.2 Common locations of cargo thefts. Thieves can strike anywhere.

book will follow through with a theft at any location if the correct opportunity presents itself. Location rarely concerns organized groups; the important factor is the point at which the load is vulnerable and they have an opening to do their work.

This is a key point for industries to understand and thus step up protection in their own facilities and control circumstances of when and where drivers stop while carrying high-value loads. These thefts can and do occur quickly. A victimized driver who did not apply the locks or immobilization equipment because he was only going to be away from the rig for a few minutes has no valid excuse. It is important to stress the awareness of this known risk to every employee level in the supply chain. Cargo vulnerability is also pushing the industry to look for security applications that do not have to rely on drivers. Future security may rely on remote wireless communication technology integrated into in-transit units to control and operate tracking, locking, and engine shut-down hardware.

The willingness of cargo thieves to focus their efforts on carrier facilities and secured lots where they are more likely to confront a variety of security measures speaks volumes about their perception of the risk-to-reward ratio of cargo crime. While they do not intend to confront anyone in the course of committing a crime, they are still bold enough to move into highly controlled and sometimes secure areas to do their dirty work. Whether moving covertly or acting boldly, the thieves frequently operate "under the noses" of unsuspecting company employees and truck stop patrons. Whether a driver is planning to leave a loaded rig unattended for 2 minutes or 2 days, the security and immobilization devices must be deployed. Drivers must be made aware of current risks, especially if they are carrying the targeted commodities shown in Table 1.1.

When Thefts Occur

Figure 1.3 shows what supply chain stakeholders and law enforcement have long suspected: cargo thieves are most active over weekends, regardless of the time of year. The bump in activity on Tuesdays can be attributed to extended weekends due to state and national holidays. This issue is very important to the operators of supply chain companies as it clearly shows that their facilities and in-transit loads are more heavily targeted when left unattended or where activity is minimal. Since the SC-ISAC started this analysis, the data have been consistent: weekends and 3-day holiday weekends continue to be the windows of the highest cargo theft activity. Although cargo thieves may have altered where they strike

Table 1.1   Frequently Stolen Products

Category	Items
Automotive	Tires
Beverages	Power drinks
Clothing and accessories	Clothing
Computers and peripherals	Computers
Consumer electronics	Televisions
Drugs and medical aids	Pharmaceuticals
Food	Meats and non-alcoholic beverages
Health and beauty products	Perfume
Tobacco and spirited beverages	Liquor, wine, and beer
Construction supplies	Metals
Furniture	Office furniture
Appliances	Washers and dryers
Housewares	Paper products

over the past few years, the data showing when thefts occur remained very consistent, never once showing a dissimilar result in any of the quarterly analyses conducted.

Among all the figures and data, Figure 1.3 shows the most consistent trend over the 3-year period and earlier. It clearly illustrates to the transportation security professional the huge need for each supply chain operation to fully protect its assets during weekends, and particularly over 3-day holiday weekends.

Locking down facilities is not the biggest challenge; the challenges appear during the release of freight for transit, while it is in transit, and during receipt at arrival. The risks are not always easy to fix because of variations in consignee needs, business schedules, and other factors. These vulnerabilities should be major considerations for high-value shipments. The goal should be to never allow your freight to be dropped off or left unattended. "Freight at rest is freight at risk" is

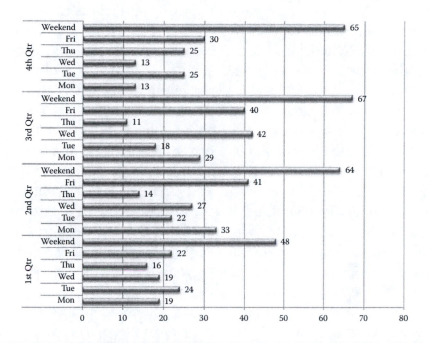

Figure 1.3   Weekends, particularly three-day weekends, are the pre-ferred theft days.

probably the most frequently used phrase in the industry. I do not know who first spoke those seven words but they serve as a very important reminder that freight should never be left at rest without adequate protection.

The most common statement of a victimized truck driver is "I was only going to be gone for a few minutes." Once you understand the methods of operations of organized theft groups we will be talking about, you will understand why both rig and freight can disappear very quickly.

What's Stolen

The commodities and specific items most often reported stolen during 2009 are certainly no strangers to our earlier analysis.

They simply confirm what we learned at the start of the analysis. The data reveal something that our analysis shows almost every quarter and every year: food is the most targeted commodity. When we look at the data for 2009 and 2010, we see that food commodities lead the way—at the top of eleven categories for eleven of the last twelve quarters. This is a result that very few persons without intimate knowledge of cargo theft information would ever presume. Most people would probably guess that consumer electronics would be number one, but they move up and down the quarterly charts much more so than food, which is the consistent leader. Different sets of criminals target food and consumer electronics, but the main issue for industry is being aware of the targeted commodities. Although the amounts of theft incidents increase in the third and fourth quarters every year, the commodity percentages are fairly consistent as shown in Figure 1.4.

When I first started in the industry, you could almost always count on a spike in theft activity in the third quarter. The reason for this spike is that around Labor Day, the high-value freight starts making its way from manufacturer to distributor to destination store so that it will be in place for "black Friday" shopping the day after Thanksgiving. Volumes in freight stay high during the third and fourth quarters, usually with the higher value freight being shipped for Christmas sales. When you look at all the data, you will see those upward trends. The freight volume increase during those quarters is very significant and it truly does affect the loss numbers. When high-value shipments involving the targeted commodities increase by a rather large percentage, adequate handling procedures often fall below the standard security requirements because of the pressure.

Cargo thieves consistently target the same commodities and specific items, essentially offering supply chain stakeholders a major page from their playbook. Knowing which commodities and products are on the target list is the most important information a supply chain operator can have. If you aren't

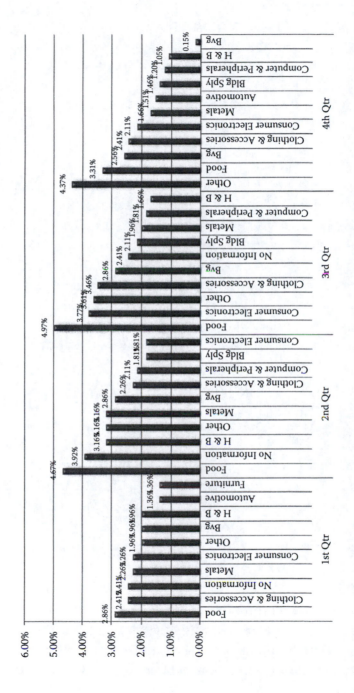

Figure1.4 Food leads the list of commodities preferred for theft during three of four quarters and eleven of the last twelve quarters.

An LTL (less than truckload) company in Houston had a problem with flat screen television shipments going to a specific consignee during the holiday season. The consignee would only take deliveries at certain times and because of some confusion between the shipper and the consignee, the LTL company was left with a large number of very high-value flat screen TVs and had to store this high-value product in trailers at its terminal yard over the Thanksgiving holiday.

An entrepreneurial employee decided to take advantage of the situation. After he finished his shift for the evening, he pulled one of the TV storage trailers from the yard to a liquor store near the terminal and called several other employees and friends to help themselves to the goods. After a large portion of the freight had been removed, he returned the trailer to the yard. When the significant shortages were discovered, I was notified and began the investigation that led to terminations and arrests of a large number of employees.

The loss was caused by dishonest employees, but the opportunity presented itself when the shipper and consignee could not coordinate the delivery of a very large amount of valuable freight. This left the carrier "in limbo" with large amounts of expensive freight that it was not equipped to store in a secure manner. In retrospect, the operations personnel could have handled the problem better. Dealing with unexpected situations and exceptions can hinder security planning if an operation is not prepared for aberrations.

working with the commodities shown in Figures 1.4 and 1.5 and Table 1.1, your threats and risk go way down. The most significant part of understanding organized cargo thieves is being cognizant of the commodities they target, desire, and pursue.

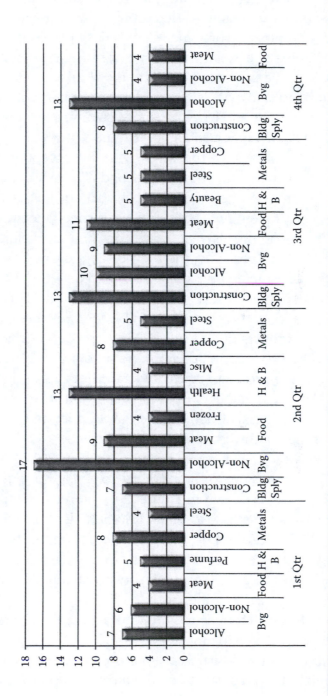

Figure 1.5   Cargo thieves desire the same products most people want.

The data covering 2009 through 2011 list the same commodities and specific items—frequently very high-value computer equipment, consumer electronics, and consumable goods. It seems that stolen items that are sought after and not expensive can be sold easily and are more difficult for law enforcement to track via serial numbers or document by other means. Figure 1.4 and Figure 1.5 show commodities that are known targets of organized cargo criminals.

Food commodities led the way—with the exception of the fourth quarter, when they ranked second. There are many things to learn from the three years of data and the 2011 charts. You can identify certain cycles for specific commodities. For example, metals cycle based on their market costs. If the price of copper is up, the theft of copper increases. In an analysis of targeted and stolen commodities in California, a California Highway Patrol (CHP) analysis noted, "Food, electronics, and clothing continue to be the most sought after stolen products due to the ease of resell and value of return on the product. In addition, the inability to identify and recover the products efficiently and effectively once distributed. As stated earlier, we saw a significant increase in construction materials (roofing material, lumber, tile, metal, piping) in the southwest area. Most of the other products stayed relative to the previous years" (Hawkins 2011).

The California study is almost a mirror image of our findings nationwide as shown in Figure 1.4. The most significant increase (that seems now to be an anomaly) is the "other" category in the SC-ISAC report ranking number one in the fourth quarter. The "miscellaneous" category in the California report jumped to third in 2011. This may show a change in targeting strategies by the cargo criminals.

We need to watch this area for several more quarters to see whether it is a changing factor. In the past, cargo criminals did not show a desire to prey upon consolidated loads or mixed freight because variations limited their control over the products they were seeking. The increase in thefts of "other" and "miscellaneous" items indicates that they are willing to hit these loads now but the pattern seems to show that they are targeting mixed loads that they know have value. In other words, they seek loads from high-value shippers or warehouse type store distribution centers that probably contain high-value products that can be resold easily. Beverage loads continue to be desirable targets, particularly power and non-alcoholic drinks. They too are easy to sell and hard to trace and track by law enforcement. Table 1.1 lists the most frequently stolen products over a three-year span.

Conclusion

After looking at the data for 2009 through 2011 and the 2011 charts from the SC-ISAC, we now have an idea about three of the five cargo crime tenets. The *what, where*, and *when* have been identified from analysis of the charts. The *what* consists of commodities preferred by cargo thieves. Remember that with organized cargo theft, the *what* is the most important factor. Real cargo thieves know the products they are after and target those specific commodities as part of their method of operation, which we will talk more about in Chapter 3. No matter what the mode of freight transportation, the listed commodities represent the first line of products the thieves will target. The same principle also applies to internal thieves working in consolidation units. Their growth from simple pilferage to targeting pallets or greater quantities will be based on *what* the involved commodity is.

The *where* issue is detailed in the charts showing states where most thefts occur. Once again, the actual reporting may be somewhat skewed by the fact that the areas most frequently cited have cargo task forces or industry security councils that focus on the cargo crime issue. These entities tend to promote much more regional participation in information gathering and sharing. Also, because of the methods of operations of organized cargo thieves, thefts may not occur in the same state where the origin distribution center is located or the shipment originated. We will cover this in Chapter 3 also. As the participation in data gathering and information sharing continues to grow, the statistics will become even more consistent and pinpoint the changes of methods of criminals through better data analysis.

No real consistency has been demonstrated in connection with types of locations from which cargoes are stolen and specific types of crime scenes. Crime scene frequency bounces back and forth from truck stop to parking lot, to carrier facility. The main point garnered from charts and reports is to go one step further and understand that location is not as important as the fact that any location where a rig and cargo are left unattended and unsecured is vulnerable.

The *when* factor remains consistent with most activity occurring on weekends and during 3-day holiday weekends. Cargo thieves like to operate when fewer people are around and when buildings are left to the protection of alarms and other systems that can be beaten or manipulated. This fact is also important when an operation releases freight to carriers. To prevent them from dropping loaded trailers or leaving complete rigs unattended during these down times, the shippers must plan the pick-up, travel time, and service due date to avoid circumstances that allow drivers time to drop trailers or leave their rigs unattended.

For an operator in the supply chain, the information from the charts in this chapter produces a pretty clear picture. When we add the information in upcoming chapters about the criminal methods of organized and opportunistic cargo thieves, the focus will become clear as to what must be done to protect freight, especially of cargoes of high value, in transit or storage during its move from manufacturer to distribution center and on to final destination.

Chapter 2

Modes of Freight Transportation

Introduction

Freight is moved by many different means. Each mode of freight transportation presents different challenges related to theft and loss. To understand the big picture of theft within the transportation industry, you must first understand how freight moves. Companies have many choices, based on their needs. When looking at the different transportation modes, a company must determine which one provides the transit times, service, cost-efficiency, and security its freight needs. Depending on the commodity to be shipped and the volume of freight to be moved, a shipper must consider several factors and choices. Cost is usually the main factor followed by special considerations needed to make the shipper's customers or buyers happy by meeting service due dates, preventing loss and damage, and being a responsive business partner.

Freight Modalities

Most of the information and figures reviewed in Chapter 1 relate to full truckload thefts, but industries use other types of shipping modalities as described below.

Full truckload (FTL)—As the name indicates, the FTL is one trailer load of freight belonging to one shipper, for example, a 53-foot van loaded with product from a single owner. FTL shipping is the movement of large amounts of standardized cargo, generally the amount necessary to fill an entire semitrailer or intermodal container. A truckload carrier is a trucking company that generally contracts an entire trailer load to a single customer. The big advantage is that freight shipped by FTL carriers is rarely handled or involved in a consolidation while en route. This eliminates internal theft to a degree but FTL loads are still subject to theft from external non-employee criminals. This mode is targeted by the commodity carried and the loaded rig being left unattended. Most driver give-ups occur with this mode, especially when non-company drivers are used. We will talk about driver give-ups and truck-stop crime in the next chapter.

Less than truckload (LTL)—This mode transports relatively small freight that is too big for parcel carriers and too small to go with a full trailer load. LTL carriers use semitrailers that are typically between 28 and 53 feet long. They fill the trailers with freight, usually pallet size, from many customers to make such transportation economical. This mode uses a consolidation system to move each customer's freight from origin to destination. This consolidation system means that the freight requires handling several times while in transit, depending on the shipment route. This system of freight transportation is very controlled when it comes to the drivers and the long-haul portion of the operation. The advantages of this mode are control and the flexibility of the system for a shipper. The move may take a little more time because of the consolidation process, but it can service a shipper needing to distribute to multiple locations quickly. The consolidation process is a security risk because product must be handled several times while in transit. Due to the need for consolidation in the LTL system, most thefts are committed by employees or involve employee collusion with outside parties.

Air cargo and freight forwarding—This is the transportation of freight by air conveyance. There are several true air carriers, such as UPS and FedEx, that use their own dedicated cargo planes to move freight. This segment of the freight transportation industry involves many international shipments. The strengths of this mode are the shipment transit times and the security during moves. The weakness and most thefts occur during the loading or unloading phase, usually when cartage agents and contractors are used. Many freight forwarders buy space on cargo or passenger planes for their customers shipments. After they secure space, they sell it to customers for freight movement. In this mode, both the companies and freight forwarders face most of their theft risks during consolidation. Trucks are required at both ends of an air shipment for pick-up and delivery. Also, much of the freight-forwarding shipping is done by truck and the truck segments create the most opportunities for problems and exceptions.

Intermodal rail and ocean shipping—Freight is transported in an intermodal container or vehicle, (trailer) via truck, rail, and/or ship without any handling of the freight during mode changes. The reduced cargo handling improves security and lessens the chances for pilferage and losses. Full container load (FCL) and less than container load (LCL) shipping are involved. Rail shipments are vulnerable during movement or in the switch yards. Shipping containers on a ship, because of the way they are loaded, are less subject to in-transit risks but have the same issues as other types of freight once they reach port and begin moving by truck. Rail and ocean modes are usually secure and economical means of shipping.

Warehousing and third party logistic providers (3PLs)—These firms provide outsourced services to customers for some or all of their supply chain functions. 3PLs typically specialize in integrated operation, warehousing, and transportation services that can be customized to the needs of a particular customer. Warehousing is the performance of administrative and physical functions associated with storage of goods and materials (receipt, identification, inspection, verification, storing, and retrieval) and issuing products. Warehousing must secure the building, product, and its operating yard. A 3PL usually selects the transportation carriers for its operation and, depending on its needs, will use FTL, LTL or other mode carriers based on its requirements.

Parcel shipping or package delivery—Packages (parcels) or high-value mail items are transported as single shipments. While such service is provided by most government postal services, parcel shipping is the prime business of private companies like UPS and FedEx. Small package shipping and delivery is a consolidated service that moves low-weight parcels and single shipments. Using government postal services or private entities is usually just a preference or based on pricing. Actually, many private companies service or supplement postal shipping and distribution. This form of shipping is definitely a consolidation mode with most risk of theft present during handling stages.

When I worked for the transportation conglomerate, it utilized all of these types of transportation modes except for small parcel, rail, and ocean shipping. The company used trucks to pick up and deliver freight to rail yards and ports and participated in the consolidation of freight from these locations. The company had a security department that had a loss reporting process in place that assigned loss investigations over the entire enterprise to the security managers by region. I was assigned cases involving different types of theft and methods and occurred during all transportation modes. I kept a case log that acted as my personal archive and record. The ongoing record allowed me to make many determinations as to the types of suspects, internal or external, and criminal methods of operation.

Cargo Crime by Modality

Cargo crime methods and theft risk vary by mode. Incidents can be similar, slightly different, or wholly dissimilar challenges. The most inherent risk in the FTL mode is theft of a complete rig or a fully loaded dropped trailer. During my 10-year stint working for a logistic service provider, our 3PL company that handled warehousing and transportation for a large computer company suffered numerous full truckload thefts.

Pilferage is not as prevalent with FTL movements with the exception of trailer burglaries when the rigs are parked at truck stops, rest areas, unsecured lots, or on streets. Burglaries frequently occur while a driver is asleep in a rig or when the unit is left unattended. Theft from external sources is much more likely with this mode of transportation. Although you may find employee collusion, about 85% of criminal activity in FTL is from external nonemployee criminals. The 15% internal activity can usually be traced directly to driver involvement. The organized gangs that target specific commodities usually commit thefts against FTL carriers.

The LTL mode of transportation removes the cargo criminal's ability to choose and control the product when stealing a completely loaded trailer because freight of all kinds may be aboard. Pilferage committed by employees is a far more prevalent problem in the LTL mode because of the consolidation process and the number of times shipments are handled. Exception reports involving theft in the LTL mode indicate that about 85% of the theft is from internal sources and greater problems can be expected when organized employee theft rings evolve.

When I provided security and investigation services to our carrier companies within my region, two of the larger aggregated thefts of freight were committed by organized employee theft rings. Employees of LTL companies learn how to manipulate the system to be able to remove large amounts of freight from shipping lanes or terminals. Documentation and supervisory control are extremely important in this or any other mode that involves consolidation. Several full trailer load thefts from an LTL carrier occurred in my region but each time we recovered the majority of the freight. Stealing fully loaded LTL trailers is a blind luck proposition unless you have collusion from inside. As Forrest Gump said, "Life is like a box of chocolates, you never know what you're gonna get."

All modes of transportation that utilize facilities and yards must secure those areas. These locations for every mode are constant targets of criminals looking for easy marks. Since all freight transportation modes begin and end with moves by truck, all providers are vulnerable to truck crime and should ensure adequate crime prevention. Truck, trailer, and container security should be the number one task of every entity involved in moving freight. People in the industry always say that "freight at rest is freight at risk." The slogan applies to every part of the supply chain. Understanding this simple phrase can assist you in preparing an effective security plan for each mode.

Rail shipments present their own unique challenges. Even though they have the same task of securing their yards, terminals, and trucks with trailers or containers, they are also known to face organized gangs of thieves who target their trains while in transit, especially in the west and desert southwest part of the United States. The Conrail Boyz targeted Norfolk Southern and CSX trainloads in the New Jersey and New York area. Rail thefts are many times not discovered until a car arrives at the last destination yard; the location where the crime or breach occurred is unknown. Without that information, making a police report is extremely difficult and a follow-up investigation without a crime scene is almost impossible. Railroads have their own sworn police forces but they deal with miles and miles of territory and the need to secure exchange and switching yards in many very tough urban areas.

The majority of air cargo theft involves pilfering, theft at or from a consolidation point, or during loading or unloading of the cargo hold area of a plane. It usually involves internal or contracted employees who pilfer shipment pallets. As noted above, all operating locations, terminals, and distribution centers face the same issues of security in their yards and during truck moves to and from the airport.

True warehousing operations also see pilfering during storage, loading, and unloading. Warehouse managers must look at all of the same problems discussed above but also need to put solid layered security in place. Warehousing operations are subject to internal risk from employee theft and pilferage and also face risks of burglaries of their storage facilities by external criminals.

The parcel shipping mode presents all the risks cited above and then some. Because of volume, size of the freight, and value of some single shipments, this mode provides security practitioners a true challenge in every way.

As we move through later chapters, remember how each mode operates and how selecting the correct mode for cargo movement is an important step for shippers and their commodities. Providing security for specific commodities while in transit can be accomplished more easily with some transportation modes than others. Depending on what your requirements are, using the right mode can be the first step to providing a secure shipping solution for your product.

The accountability for keeping goods safe during transit and in storage lies completely with the management of transporters and manufacturers. As goods travel through these various modes of transportation, legal accountability changes. It usually lies in the hand of the company in possession of the goods when an exception occurs although responsibility is not always that easy to determine. Understanding freight movement and claims procedures along with cargo law is very important to shippers if they are going to obtain indemnity.

Conclusion

Is one mode safer than another? The answer depends on several factors. Picking the mode for your commodity is as important as picking the carrier. Once you understand how different groups target commodities, how to choose specific modes for certain shipments will make more sense. Do you want your cargo handled fewer times? Do you not want a full truckload of your product at risk?

In addition to cost realities, you have other issues to consider when making your decision. Once you determine a mode, you can pick a carrier. You should also base that choice on how a carrier handles security in its company and for its shippers. A chosen carrier should have a dedicated security department with written security and recovery plans and the ability to execute both. As I noted in Chapter 1, moving a box, pallet, or truckload from point A to point B can sometimes be more complex than expected. In the next chapter, we discuss the groups that target the industry and the methods they use. The information should allow you to make educated decisions about modes and the risks attached to them.

Chapter 3

Perpetrators of Cargo Crime

Introduction

When I first ventured into the transportation world from the public law enforcement sector and started learning and applying transportation security techniques in a real-life scenario over a multistate area for a multimode company, I saw first-hand the risks and threats to this business from inside and out. My region originally consisted of five southwest states and Mexico. Over time, it grew to involve seven states.

The business units I oversaw included every mode discussed in Chapter 2 except intermodal rail, ocean, and parcel shipping. We utilized truck operations to and from rail and ocean ports but I did not have security responsibilities for freight while it was actually on rails or on a ship. I quickly learned what issues were relevant to my area versus what the regional security managers (RSMs) in the other regions faced.

Most activities in my region, related to our LTL operations by both our union and nonunion carriers. Within the first month of my employment, I was introduced to a major internal theft ring that operated in our union LTL operation in

Houston, Texas. My predecessor RSM started an investigation and identified many of the participants. These employees had long been targeting the freight of a client that shipped computer ink cartridges. The ring started with a few boxes and progressed to taking full pallets. I learned that the shipper placed 72 cartons on each pallet and each carton contained 100 ink jet cartridges. The cartridges retailed for about $30 each, so each pallet was a very expensive shipment.

An investigative plan had been devised wherein this type of freight was cut off from traveling to or consolidating at this terminal. A baited pallet was going to be added into the system at a time when the employees known to be involved were on duty so that it would be stolen and then could be tracked to an off-company site or to a "fence." As with most plans, an unexpected activity changed the plan of action. A few days before the planned bait freight activity, an unexpected return shipment involving eight pallets of the same customer's freight was shipped into the terminal and stolen on a Sunday by several of the theft ring employees. The eight pallets were all on the same trailer. We later were able to determine that it was pulled from the yard by an employee who was supposed to be taking empty trailers to the rail yard. The theft happened on a Sunday and I was notified early Monday morning that the freight was missing.

Since we had already set up the bait operation with law enforcement for the upcoming maneuver and shared suspected employee and other information, a call to the police allowed a quick response to the location of a previously identified fence and suspects. Police observed a large rental box truck parked in front of the fence location. Within minutes after the police placed the vehicle under surveillance, two additional persons arrived and three suspects drove the box truck to a private public rental warehouse where they started off-loading the stolen ink. Subsequently, two employees and the fence were arrested; all of the freight was recovered along with stolen property from several previous thefts. The investigation identified at least six involved employees.

This was a huge learning experience early on in my transportation career. These employee/thieves were organized and very good at their scheme but, to our benefit greed overcame them. We will talk about these types of theft methods later. Perpetrators of cargo crime may be a huge crew of external bandits or a group of internal collusive employees. Let's look at some organized thieves that target full truckload shipments so we can understand their methods and operations.

Organized Cargo Criminals

Full Truckload

While I was dealing with internal crimes in my area, my company became responsible for the transportation and warehousing of a major computer manufacturer through a contract with our 3PL (third party logistic) company. The warehousing and transportation origin was set up in the state of Virginia, which was not in my region of direct responsibility. But as the business ramped up, we started experiencing full truckload thefts from this location.

Our RSM in that region and another who was assigned as a liaison for that account started following up on theft activities. They quickly learned that the equipment involved in the thefts was recovered without the cargo in the vicinities of Hialeah, Florida, and Macon, Georgia. When the RSMs spoke with law enforcement in those areas, they learned that empty rigs were commonly found in Hialeah and Macon after full truckloads were stolen around the country. The Miami-Dade Police Department's Tactical Operations Multi-Agency Cargo Anti-Theft Squad (TOMCATS) unit is dedicated to the commercial vehicle and cargo theft problem as part of the department's

Robbery Division. During a conference with the TOMCATS Task Force, our company investigators learned much about how these organized cargo criminals operated.

The group is made up of mostly South Floridians of Cuban descent. Many have extensive criminal records indicating all types of crimes. Many were taught by cargo theft veterans that this activity presents low risk and produces high rewards. They know that if they do not use force or traffic narcotics in their crimes, they will not receive harsh punishments if apprehended because their offenses are treated as property crimes by the courts. Although this concept varies around the country, it applies to most jurisdictions. The TOMCATS know that criminal crews have most of the property fenced or committed to be sold before they even commit their crimes and often target their theft by commodity and brand.

The scenario starts when the criminals and their buyers decide on a product. Once a product is decided as a possible target, an Internet search of the manufacturer is performed with the intent of learning where its manufacturing or distributing sites are located. When they have this information through Internet search or by other means, a team of thieves set out to the selected location. Usually a minimum of about four will travel to the city, rent several vehicles, and start thorough surveillance of the location. This surveillance will gather information about hours of operation, access control of people and vehicles, and physical security measures including guards, alarms, cameras, and other devices. The perpetrators will study the configuration of the building and note storefront entrances and guard access at the vehicle gates. After understanding the operation of the facility, they will start following the commercial vehicles as they leave the facility. They will note the types of seals or locks on the trailers; this information aids thieves to determine the values of the contained loads. By following the commerce from the location, they can find other local distribution warehouses and operation locations that could become future targets for other truck thefts or high-value warehouse burglaries.

After they complete their intelligence gathering at a targeted location, their plan to take down a vehicle in transit goes into effect. When a fully loaded tractor trailer leaves a location under the correct conditions, the thieves will fall in behind the unit, start the surveillance, and wait for the driver to provide them with an opportunity. Whether the driver goes 20 miles or 200, they continue the shadowing until the unit is stopped and left unattended. When that happens, within a short time, usually in fewer than 90 seconds, the criminal team will take the entire rig and escape. They can steal most rigs quickly using master keys that may be purchased on the Internet or by using ignition pullers or ignition jumpers, depending on the type of tractor.

Before 2007, theft perpetrators headed directly south to Florida. They would immediately disable the access control GPS devices and go to their fencing location to off-load the stolen goods and dump the equipment nearby. Police then had about a 16-hour window to have any chance of recovering the cargo and, in most cases, it was not recovered.

Since then, both law enforcement and the industry have acted to respond more effectively to this method of operation and the thieves have also changed their procedures to circumvent the efforts. Many high-value shippers have started using covert cargo tracking GPS equipment within shipments. Law enforcement in Florida has installed license plate readers (LPRs) at state border inspection sites. These actions have led thieves to change their methods somewhat. They continue to use the same methods to target the loads. However, after committing a theft, they drive the rig to a nearby location such as a truck stop, rest area, or mall where it does not look out of place, then leave it there under surveillance to see whether law enforcement responds. If no response is seen in a few hours, they replace the tractor with a clean (not stolen) unit and have been known to paint over logos on trailers.

We are also seeing a new phenomenon. Empty trailers are not all found in Florida. They are now found in many areas of the country where the crews have small splinter operating groups working areas such as New Jersey, Kentucky, and northern Texas around Dallas.

An analysis of cargo theft by the Supply Chain Information Sharing and Analysis Center (SC-ISAC) confirms these activities and changes in the operations of cargo criminals. In tracking recoveries, we have definitely seen the equipment change-outs and differences in equipment recovery locations for about two years now. Having this knowledge about the changes in methods has assisted in several recoveries lately. When a cargo theft occurs, if the complainant company can advise the responding law enforcement agencies about the known methods currently used by the thieves, the recovery probability increases as the search can be focused. No matter what product is involved, knowledge about the *who, what, where, how,* and *why* makes the response to the problem more manageable and brings a better chance of success. Later in this book we will talk about recovery plans. Not understanding the methods of cargo theft predators will affect the strength of a recovery plan.

The cargo theft crews in South Florida are not a "gang" in the normal nomenclature of organized crime. They do not operate like the Costa Nostra with a known boss and a circle of lieutenants. Detective Willie Morales, a veteran of the Miami-Dade Police Department TOMCATS, stated that he would consider them "a loose-knit group of crews who use the same methods of operation, work with the same fencing organizations, and intermingle in different criminal ventures when the need arises."

As our internal investigators worked on the FTL thefts from our 3PL client, they developed a spreadsheet that listed over 250 persons of interest and potential suspects. This information and other investigations led to a geographical area, mostly by the recovery of the empty equipment and the common knowledge of the theft activity. These crews are formidable foes who are very good at what they do. The key is realizing that the target of their theft is based on the commodity. If you are a full truckload carrier of any of the targeted commodities discussed in Chapter 1, you need to understand that the risk of theft in transit is much higher than if you are carrying less desirable products. By knowing how these thieves operate, a provider of supply chain services can set up security and recovery plans that are likely to be effective. Security and prevention plans require driver awareness programs and a support mechanism for drivers who notice suspicious activity while in transit.

Fictitious or Fraudulent Pick-Ups

The newest players in this space are cargo criminals who use identity theft to pursue their cargo theft activities. As with every other aspect of life, the Internet has changed the way that industries and regulators handle the business of transportation. With the advent of freight boards and online registration for almost anything, cargo criminals have jumped through the industry and government loopholes to commit thefts. Currently, criminals are setting up fictitious trucking companies using the identities of unsuspecting individuals or stealing the identities of legitimate registered carriers.

Recently, a carrier was established in the name of a Houston man who attended a truck driving school. The company was established with the DOT, and insured and registered as a business entity by the state, apparently all online—without any official ever actually seeing anyone involved with the company. Once established, the company registered with several transportation brokerage companies and started bidding on loads posted on freight boards. During a 2-day period, the company made eight freight pick-ups in seven states and not one of the shipments was ever delivered.

The involved shipments contained various commodities including food and building supplies. Upon investigation, authorities learned that the individual whose identity was stolen did not know he had a trucking company in his name. The location for the company was found to be a rented mail drop box business and all the registration information was falsified. The company registration on the DOT Safersys website indicated a one-power unit company that made eight pick-ups in 2 days. As of this writing, none of the freight has ever been recovered.

This type of activity shows that it is critical for each shipper and brokerage company to take steps to protect its operation. The days of quick sign-up and faxing applications to a truck stop should be over. If companies continue to operate as they did when the Internet boards were first created, they are victims in waiting. We will talk about solutions later in the book but we need a further look at the group that seems to be behind this latest innovation in cargo theft.

Since this is a new phenomenon, investigation is starting to point to a loosely organized group of Eastern Europeans operating from North Hollywood, California. Private investigators have played a significant role in identifying these suspects and California law enforcement is investigating the activities and beginning to develop intelligence about the group and its methods.

I spoke with Jeff Hall, a private investigator with Transit Risk Management, and Randy Ferguson of Ferguson Investigations. They are close friends and associates through the industry councils. They both confirmed the evidence of an Armenian group in North Hollywood as a major player but they added that others are involved also. Randy is currently working on some fraudulent pick-ups (thefts) made by a known carrier. The loads were not delivered. The carrier claims that he did not receive the load, but the evidence seems to prove otherwise. The carrier claims that someone stole his identity and is fraudulently making these pick-ups.

Randy noted that getting the DOT to investigate and pull the operating authorities of bogus companies and companies operating illegally has been a real problem. Jeff and Randy have been working with the Los Angeles Police Department BADCATS group on these issues to identify the participants but because the thefts occur across the country in many different jurisdictions, obtaining investigative information and prosecuting thieves is a slow and difficult process.

Another way to profit from identity theft is to take on the identity of a current legitimate registered carrier. By using the same freight boards and changing company contact numbers, thieves bid on loads through unsuspecting brokerage agents who assign the loads. The company wins the bid, the pick-up is made, and the freight is never delivered. After the service due day is past, when the shipper and consignee start looking for the freight, a call to the legitimate carrier shows that it did not bid on the load or pick it up.

You now know three ways in which identity theft works into the equation with shipment theft. Knowing who is picking up your freight and obtaining driver and vehicle information during a pick-up is now more important than ever. This minimal information at least gives you an investigation starting point even though the license of the pick-up driver may also be fraudulent. Knowing your contacts and confirming information at the front end are the best bets to prevent being victimized by this method. Remember, this crime does not involve the recovery of the empty units to assist in identifying the suspects or the area where fences operate.

High-Value Warehouse Burglaries

Earlier we spoke about full truckload thefts, and discussed South Florida crews that specialize in that activity. The same groups are behind many high-value warehouse burglaries. So we now know the *who*. Let's look at some of the other information. Just as we spoke about the patience of these thieves and the steps they follow for in-transit thefts, we see the same factors in warehouse burglaries. Once thieves select a target warehouse, many times from in-transit surveillance activity, they will conduct the same type of survey on a target warehouse to become familiar with its operation. They will determine hours of operation, the physical security at the location, and the arrivals and departures of employees, vendors, deliveries, and other truck traffic. By watching the location, monitoring activities, and learning what is normal, the perpetrators can devise a plan to gain entry and be able to stay inside the location for a long time without being discovered. These suspects are not using smash-and-grab tactics; they plan to enter the operation, select the property they want, and make a huge haul. To do this, they must take control of the building, alarm, and security features. They must have a plan for removing large amounts of property and not being detected during the operation.

During their surveillance, the thieves will try to determine the alarm company and see whether they can gain entry via use of a code. If a warehouse has a storefront and they observe employees enter and use an alarm pad, they can plant a camera outside the storefront window in an attempt to obtain an employee's code. I have seen a TOMCATS training video in which thieves placed cameras in plants and ashtrays on the front porch of a location in an attempt to obtain the video of an alarm code. They have been known to observe the first employee enter a warehouse in the morning and watch the employee make the alarm pad entry.

Since alarm company information is frequently posted in a window, the thieves immediately phone the warehouse using a spoof app showing the alarm company name on the caller ID. When a warehouse employee answers, the caller explains that the alarm has been triggered and was not cleared via the pad. When the employee explains that the code was entered, the caller asks for the code. If the employee provides it, the thieves now have a code to clear the alarm.

If after all the surveillance and chicanery, they still have no easy way to get into the warehouse, they will take action to set off the alarm to time and monitor the law enforcement response. When they are ready to commit the offense, they will often act to set the alarm off several times until law enforcement quits responding and determine whether a company stakeholder will respond. If they finally see no activity after alarms, they will make their move.

Sometimes thieves cut all power and phone lines to a building. Usually they are known to make roof entry or sometimes cut through bay doors, but once inside they will seek the control box for the alarm and disable the whole system. While all this is being done, look-outs strategically placed with scanners and two-way radios watch for the police or anyone else approaching the site. When they have completed the entry and feel confident that they outmaneuvered the system and feel safe, they will start gathering product and moving it to the dock for loading onto large trailers. They may even use the warehouse's forklifts and other equipment to assist in their efforts. Once they have the product in loading position, they will call in associates to bring tractor trailers to the location and back them to the dock. Most of the units have usually been stolen from nearby locations. Once the units are loaded with the goods, the thieves will leave with several trailer loads of products.

We see many of these types of offenses over 3-day weekends when warehouse thieves commonly strike. Two recent offenses occurred, one in the Dallas area that involved a warehouse hit for the third time. The thieves took three trailer loads of flat screen televisions and left empty stolen tractor trailers at the location after leaving abruptly when they thought police were responding. Another incident involved at least one of the same suspects (matched by DNA) in a pharmaceutical warehouse burglary in Connecticut. The suspects escaped with approximately $76 million worth of goods. The method of operations (MO) in both cases was almost identical and both occurred during 3-day weekends.

We will look at solutions for these types of break-ins in a later chapter. Employee training and constant awareness are required for a facility not to become a victim of some of the alarm code tricks of crooks. Also, using the correct physical security equipment can make the thieves' MO much less effective.

Opportunistic Cargo Theft

Just about every major city in the United States has areas of major industrial influence and heavy trucking activity. Truck terminals and truck stops are very seldom the centerpieces of a city and are in fact usually in section of municipalities that are less than desirable. Truck stops are generally known as havens for drugs, prostitution, and other illicit activities. It is unfortunate that this is the case. Because of this reality, operators must consider the true environment around their businesses. Obviously, some are worse than others and not all present the huge problems that can be expected at certain big-city locations. It is important to understand the dynamics of opportunistic theft.

People who use truck stops and areas near them must understand that this environment subjects drivers to persons offering illegal services or favors in return for the cargo in their trucks. Predators work these areas and look for dropped trailers in unsecured lots or areas that make for easy pickings. Most opportunistic thieves who work this way have buyers who will quickly give them ten cents on the dollar for anything they bring. These vultures prey on drop lots, truck yards, and truck stops and look for the easy mark. If they steal a trailer and pull it a few miles, and check the load and find it is product they do not want, they will just leave it and search for something better.

In some local jurisdictions, the district attorney may not consider a driver's give-up of a load in exchange for drugs or prostitution a crime. This is completely unfair to the transportation industry. A driver give-up is a crime, not a civil case. Those same district attorneys will prosecute internal thieves in other industries for much smaller losses but will not prosecute a truck driver who exchanges thousands of dollars of freight for drugs or sex. This lack of support from the justice system is totally wrong. Investigation should be warranted for any illegal activity. A blanket statement of prosecutorial denial for any incident deemed a driver give-up is totally irresponsible and allows this type of activity to continue unchecked.

Many opportunistic groups have their own tractor units and troll the drop yards continuously for unsecured trailers. Companies and drivers need to be aware of these types of activities and all drops of trailers must conform to secure guidelines.

One other activity of opportunistic groups is burglarizing parked rigs. These thefts frequently happen at truck stops or industrial areas where trucks park and wait to make deliveries. When the trucks cannot park in secured areas and are forced to park or wait in areas outside high-value distribution warehouses, they may be watched by thieves looking to make a quick hit on a trailer full of product. Many drivers go to sleep in their rigs and never know of a breach until the next day. Many hazards await drivers who do not understand the risks of a neighborhood, the value of the products they carry, and the skills of predators looking for an easy mark.

Internal Theft Rings: Consolidation

Whenever freight is handled, at rest, or between conveyances, it is always at high risk. When I worked for as large transportation consortium, many of the incidents I investigated were internal thefts usually occurring at consolidation points while the freight was handled. The company had a loss reporting system that keyed regional security managers into shortages. The system worked much like a law enforcement offense-reporting structure and follow-up assignment to detectives. The system notified RSMs of losses that crossed through their regions and they were assigned primary responsibility for follow-up of the losses. The system allowed RSMs to file, sort, and archive information so that patterns and trends could be identified. Freight paperwork is very detailed and usually allows investigators to pinpoint where an exception or problem occurred. Through company documents such as bills of lading, manifests, line-haul records, and final delivery receipts, the paths of shipments can be totally recreated and a record of every movement, handler, and driver can be established.

As a regional security manager, I was able to establish that about 85% of the thefts occurring during shipments requiring consolidation involved a company employee as the thief or in collusion with other thieves. Internal theft rings can create huge losses.

Large LTL companies and other transportation entities that utilize consolidation face this problem fairly often. Sometimes a problem arises from one employee involved in petty pilfering or a loss can be caused by several employees who form major theft rings. I had the occasion to investigate many losses arising from both situations. When a ring of thieves starts working within an organization and gains momentum, they can really stack up the exceptions. As with all good police evidence, shipment information tells a story and eventually points to the problem area.

People outside the shipping may be amazed that both small portions of shipments are stolen and full pallets of merchandise also disappear. In a theft situation, you must consider the operation affected and all of its moving parts. The LTL operation often represents the perfect situation for thieves to victimize. In large terminals that experience the most problems with this type of activity, a city pick-up and delivery operation may coexist with a line-haul break bulk freight assembly center (FAC). These two activities on the same dock assist the dishonest to hide their actions. If you have ever been on an LTL dock when it is at the peak of an operation, it looks like an army of ants on a mound. It can be very difficult to tell which ongoing activity is dishonest. This is where the handling of paperwork becomes a great benefit as it allows an RSM to tie together the handlers of the freight with sections of the dock, times, and other pertinent information. Full pallets that disappear usually go right out of the gate on a city unit. The freight is taken and loaded onto an accomplice's trailer. During his runs around the city, he drops it off at an agreed-upon location and the unauthorized delivery is conducted almost like an authorized one.

The numbers of employees involved and their levels in the organization determine the extents of losses. The two worse cases usually involve a supervisory-level employee or misguided dock workers and drivers who can be prodded by a fence (buyer) who provides cash upon delivery. In my career, both occasions occurred and the losses were pretty significant before we were able to identify the thieving employees and halt the activity.

When internal thefts start at a location, operational supervisors often suggest that the problems started about the same time as a new employee came on the job. However, if a company experiences losses of large amounts of freight on pallets, the cause is most likely a longer term employee. I would say most of those involved in the major theft activities I investigated had tenures averaging at least four years.

After looking at the current known risks of cargo in the supply chain, we also must remember that the securing of facilities, vehicles, and other business property in addition to cargo is also a huge business imperative for all modes. Meeting all of the security needs for this type of business operation can be a huge undertaking. The LTL operation I worked for had 432 locations around the United States, including facilities in very large cities that handled very large operations and very remote locations where no freight was ever stored overnight. Each location had specific security needs along with the in-transit segments. The LTL mode is much different from an FTL operation and provides a much more controlled environment for drivers. The freight is seldom at rest while in transit but because of consolidation, the freight is put at some risk at every break-out point.

In one circumstance, my region suffered a slew of shortages from a smaller terminal whose biggest operation was as a major line-haul FAC break bulk point during night shifts handling major freight and large products. The terminal was in West Texas and most of the product moving from the West Coast passed through the location. One major investigative factor was that all the loads checked into the terminal FAC and left and all the shipments were short (missing cargo) at the next destination or consolidation point.

During the investigation, I gathered the records on numerous shortages of consumer electronics, computers, power tools, and appliances. The night operation was run somewhat independently of the terminal operation. It had its own supervisor and crew who worked the shift. Because of the amount of freight that came up short at the next stop down the line from this location, we decided to place the night shift operation under surveillance. I and a second investigator, Tina Weatherford, had not been in place very long when we saw an employee take an item to his car, smoke a cigarette, and return to the building. I went to the vehicle and through a hatchback window could plainly see a new case for a battery-powered drill from one of our shippers. Many of the reported shortages had been just such items. This gave us the opening we needed to confront the involved employee.

We recovered the stolen drill and began our interview with the employee. The trail led to other employees and all the way to the night supervisor. Eight employees were eventually terminated and faced criminal charges for their collusive activities. A large trailer was required to recover the property from the involved supervisor who worked in collusion with a whole shift. They would load a 28-foot trailer with the product they planned to steal during the shift, remove the trailer, and stage it on a vacant lot in a remote location east of the terminal. The employee participants visited the trailer after work and used their personal vehicles to retrieve their illicit goods. Some of the property recovered included refrigerators, lawn mowers, laptops, and tools. The whole night shift was corrupted. When deep background investigations were conducted on the group of employee thieves, several, including the supervisor, were found to have criminal records that should have prevented their hiring.

Commercial Vehicle Smuggling

When a business is involved in moving product or using others to move its product via commercial vehicles, it is vulnerable to external forces and their own employees who can use that commerce stream for purposes beyond the original intent. In the supply chain, we see the smuggling of people, contraband, and unauthorized freight. All the modes of transportation are subject to smuggling activity. Each mode of legitimate commerce must try to prevent specific types of smuggling activities. The industry will always be vulnerable to stowaways, contraband, and unauthorized freight.

Later in the book we will take a close look at how contraband is placed in commercial shipping lanes. I have seen contraband in LTL and FTL trucking and air transport. Commercial trucking from crossing the U.S.–Mexico border is used for the transportation of illegal immigrants. These are all concerns and legitimate carriers never want to haul illegitimate freight or illegal people. The smugglers use commercial vehicles and systems so that they can move their illicit products and stay an arm's length away from the shipment. By using certain methods that we will discuss at length later in the book, they can move their product through government checkpoints, thus allowing commercial shippers to act as their unsuspecting mules.

Truck-Stop Crime

Truck stops are little cities and centers of commerce of all sorts. Truck stops provide stores, restaurants, fuel, truck maintenance facilities, showers, rest areas, and Internet load boards. They have large parking lots with spaces to accommodate many tractors and trailers. Most truck stops do not claim to provide secure parking and even forbid leaving drop trailers in their lots. Most long-term truck drivers, usually owner-operators, feel secure in these surroundings. Each truck stop has its individual appeal to drivers and they become loyal to truck stops on the routes they frequent. But each truck stop has an underbelly of crime and illicit activity.

Most big or inner city truck stops are known to have unauthorized drug dealing and prostitution activity within their confines. These criminal activities can entangle drivers who participate in drug activity and prostitution and can put the cargo in their possession at risk. This is a common problem and can even be exacerbated when law enforcement jurisdictions will not prosecute a driver who gives up his load for drugs or the entertainment from ladies of the evening. A driver with a fully loaded unit who engages in this type of activity puts himself and his freight at risk.

While I was writing this section of the book, I received a "be on the look out" (BOLO) message about a case reported in Dallas to an insurance company and to the Dallas police. The BOLO reproduced below involved a theft of tires from a driver who allowed a prostitute into his unit, as a result of which he was robbed of his load.

CARGO THEFT

Stolen cargo: American tires waiting on bill of lading

Stolen from: Flying J Truck Stop, I-20 and Bonnie View, Dallas, TX

Date stolen: 3/12/2011 at 2:30 a.m.

Details: The driver was approached in parking lot by a woman named Peaches, She asked for a ride out of the parking lot. The driver gave her a ride out of the truck stop. When she exited the tractor, 3 black males entered the tractor and forced the driver into the sleeper. They dropped the trailer and took the tractor and replaced the tires on it. They went to some location off Highway 310 in Dallas. Driver believed it was 7547 Highway 310. They also took the bill of lading and the driver gas card. One of the suspects went by nickname of "Daddy Trailer" and the trailer is still missing. Driver has tractor. The driver said the male subject left him with the tractor and drove off in an older model Impala, burgundy in color.

Law enforcement: Dallas Police Department

Report #60169Z

Source: Coughlin, J.J., 2011b

The above report leaves many questions unanswered. It is obvious to me and others who work these crimes that there is more to this incident than the information in the BOLO. I asked the Dallas Police Department to provide me with some crime statistics relating to the area where truck stops are concentrated in the South Dallas area on Interstate 20 between Interstate 45 and Interstate 35. When I requested the data, the supervisor who was going to provide me the detail, stated that the Dallas Police now make all criminal complainants from truck stops come to a station and make their reports in person. Obviously, this cuts down on reporting and skews the crime data as reporting persons may not take the extra step to file a report if a report is not vital.

The data provided was from Dallas Crime Reporting Area 4376, which includes a major truck stop and numerous truck-related businesses near Interstate 20. The reporting period they provided covered the 5 1/2 months from June 1, 2009 until November 16, 2009. During the reporting period for the area, the police listed 114 Part 1 offenses (felonies including theft, robbery, burglary, murder, rape, aggravated assault, and motor vehicle theft) of which 79 were thefts or burglaries of motor vehicles and 4 were motor vehicle thefts.

The police department also provided information for a second truck stop in that same area but in Crime Reporting Area 4375, located north of Interstate 20, just across the interstate from the other one. In that same time period, 50 Part 1 offenses occurred in Area 4375—30 thefts or burglaries of motor vehicles and 2 motor vehicle thefts. That means in a 5½ month period in and around the two truck stops and related businesses, 164 Part I offenses including 109 thefts or burglaries of motor vehicles and 6 motor vehicle thefts were reported—an average of about one major offense at each location daily. These truck stops and businesses are all at the intersection of Bonnie View Road and Interstate 20 in Dallas, on the north and south sides of the highway (Dallas PD, 2012).

The Dallas information confirms much about truck stops in big cities, especially in the states and areas identified in Chapter 1. There is also a large FTL terminal and yard on the north side of Interstate 20, just west of the one truck stop on the north side. The physical security and controls in place at the facility serve as testimony to the dangers of the area and some of the crimes that occurred on the property before installation of the necessary security features.

This Dallas Police crime report documentation did not include information about arrests for drugs and prostitution or the misdemeanor offenses reported. These statistics represent two truck stops in close proximity at an intersection in South Dallas. I believe that if we pulled these types of records from truck stops at locations where cargo thefts are prevalent, we would find much of the same criminality statistics. Many rural truck stop locations do not experience this level of crime activity, but they are known for trailer burglaries and partial load thefts. To reiterate, it is necessary for a freight operator to be aware of conditions surrounding the transit of his freight and understanding the risks when cargo is in transit.

Fencing: Where Stolen Cargo Goes

Fencing is the crime of buying and reselling stolen merchandise. The criminal codes do not call the activity "fencing," and usually call the crime receiving of stolen goods. Three legal elements are required to prove that such activity is a crime: (1) the property must be stolen, (2) the property must be received or concealed, and (3) the receiver must have knowledge that the property was stolen. The element of exchange of money is not necessary.

Most types of cargo theft involve a fencing element. The level of the fence operation changes with the level of the theft operation in most cases. The organized groups fill needs or take orders based on what a fence and his market desire. The professional crews of thieves working in organized groups probably garner a higher percentage of the value of the goods, or at least the leader of the crew does. Most stolen freight that ends up in South Florida is believed to be shipped to foreign destinations. Only a small percentage of the outbound freight leaving the country is checked and stolen freight is often shipped by carriers who are doing legitimate business and do not know that the shipper's freight has been stolen.

The opportunistic groups tend to be less selective and have little control of what they steal. In turn, they make less money—usually about ten cents on the dollar for the goods they bring to their buyers. A small-time thief pilfering from a consolidation operation usually steals small amounts of goods and may achieve a quick turn of the goods through a reliable system of pawn shops or street drug dealers. I recently solved several internal thefts through the reliable method of tying suspected employees to dock pilferages through pawn records.

We have seen incidents in which stolen freight worked itself back into legitimate commerce from the black or gray market and in each case an independent investigation would be needed to determine how that happened. It is believed that most of the fences for high-value cargo loads stolen by organized criminal groups have referral fences or master fences that move the product through their established networks to vetted and confirmed buyers and sources known to be secure from law enforcement.

A new method is e-fencing, which is the resale of stolen goods online through Craigslist, eBay, and similar e-commerce sites. This type of fencing gives thieves and receivers access to buyers they otherwise would never touch. In the cargo world, e-fending has been limited somewhat to pilferage from LTL shipments rather than from large high-value heists, but several higher echelon cargo thieves have been found using this venue recently.

Cargo thieves and fences operate at different levels. The fraudulent pick-up thieves who steal loads of meat and food along with construction and home building supplies probably use lower level fences such as store owners that sell the types of goods that have been stolen. These goods are not serialized and are very hard to trace, making their sales easy for this level of receiver. Thieves of ethnic descent frequently move goods within their own ethnic community to prevent detection.

During the writing of this book, the Carrollton Police, the Dallas Police, and District 1 State Police agents in Texas located and identified two warehouse properties that received and stored stolen goods that came from cargo thefts in the Dallas and Fort Worth areas. The product represented at least five different offenses and the eventual property recovery was in the neighborhood of $1.5 million to $2 million. The products included paints, cosmetics, and furniture. The persons linked to these operations had ties to South Florida crews and a fencing and receiving location was set up for a local splinter group operating in the area. The investigation has led to one arrest so far and the police are still trying to determine how the property was to be moved on from the fencing operation and where it was headed. This incident confirms splinter group activity in this area and is the second major group identified in this region in a year. It would be ideal to take an investigation like this one step further and trace where and by what means the stolen property is routed. This is very difficult to do without task force or federal jurisdiction involvement.

Unfortunately, due to the lack of the capabilities to commit to long-term investigation, the police investigators are limited to focusing on the thieves and not the receivers. The goal of all organized criminal enterprise investigations should be to identify the thieves and the receivers and prevent future activities. The lack of an easy outlet for illicit products will make such crimes less desirable. A thief wants to finish a job and relieve himself of stolen goods as soon as possible. In actuality, the crime of theft is not complete in a thief's mind until he completes both sides of the transaction without getting caught. In the world of organized criminals, very few successful thieves are also down-line dealers of the product. This appears to be the situation also in the world of cargo crime.

In one of the investigations I conducted and described in the introduction of this chapter, the fence was identified and interviewed by law enforcement. He confirmed his role in the crime. He advised that the transportation company employees contacted him on a Sunday, advising that they obtained eight pallets of computer ink worth $2.3 million. That afternoon, the fence met the employee thieves at a fast food restaurant and gave them the $190,000 in cash—a fine payday for the employee gang.

Not many persons I know have $190,000 lying around to complete a transaction on any day of the week. A fence contact with that kind of liquid cash can shake a transportation company to its core with losses. The worse thing that can happen to a transportation security manager is for dishonest employees to meet a fence who has access to cash and is willing to pay them for any product they bring.

Conclusion

Figures 1.1 to 1.5 in Chapter 1 provided you information about the *what*, *where*, and *when* of cargo theft. This chapter presented information on the various perpetrators of such crimes. You can now tie a few other points together. When you further analyze each theft, you can usually tie the offense to a certain type of group. Food is almost always the number one commodity on the targeted list, but is seldom the target of the South Floridian ethnic crews. Food thefts usually involve local opportunistic criminals and fraudulent pick-up artists. Electronics, pharmaceutical, and other high-value merchandise falls more to the organized South Florida crews.

Although it is not always possible to determine responsibility because many crimes are never solved, you can make valid conclusions based on where empty equipment is found and where the products or parts of the loads surface. Each group tends to specialize and operate in ways that tend to identify them to industry officials and police who analyze the activity. Most criminals who succeed in their endeavors repeat their activity using the same methods. An investigator can find method similarities, for example, the way a perpetrator acts or what he or she says during a crime. Groups are no different. Success breeds repetition and repetition breeds analysis that can identify trends, patterns, and behavior and link them to the groups we have identified.

After reviewing the characteristics of the various groups of predators who are looking to target parts of the supply chain, you should clearly understand that the industry must find ways to protect itself. It is really important to understand the risks and threats prevalent in a specific operation and take the steps necessary to have the best chance for success. As we go into Section II of this book, we will look at what steps the industry and law enforcement have taken in response to the cargo theft problem. The industry has taken the lead but must not be complacent. We should keep pushing for necessary law enforcement support and participation and legislative assistance where needed.

INDUSTRY AND LAW ENFORCEMENT RESPONSES

Chapter 4

Industry Responses

Introduction

Most people have no idea that a cargo theft problem exists. Cargo theft is a property crime that is not reported in the news media or grocery store tabloids. It is a reality that rides under the radar of most of society and does not get sufficient attention from businesses in the supply chain. Most law enforcement officers have no idea that cargo theft is an issue unless they are assigned to units that deal with it. A number of people in law enforcement and industry, when added to the Southwest Transportation Security Council (SWTSC) BOLO (be on the look-out) distribution list told me they had no idea that this type of crime was so prevalent.

Cargo theft is a well-kept secret and bringing the attention of industry and law enforcement to this type of crime has been a slow, steady push. Every initiative to carve out a new way of doing business in this industry, whether security related or otherwise, always moves at the rate of a baby step. Bringing the cargo theft reality to the attention of those who need to know has proceeded at the same pace. The best way to handle a loss situation is to deal with it and that is what the transportation industry security management has done.

The Vision

Only seven dedicated law enforcement cargo task forces exist in the United States and reside in areas where needs for such task forces exist. There are areas in the country where task forces are sorely needed but attempts to establish them have been unsuccessful. It is much more glamorous to chase serial killers, bank robbers, and other perpetrators of news-making crime. Preventing and fighting property crime is not romantic or newsworthy. Cities occasionally institute programs to thwart auto or home burglaries for a short period but the lack of excitement surrounding such crimes allows such plans to go by the wayside quickly.

When I worked for a police department and supervised a violent crime task force unit and street squad drug enforcement unit, never once did I see or hear about a cargo theft task force. Even the commercial auto theft investigators never spoke of enforcement measures focused on cargo. Cargo protection has never been a priority and only became an afterthought when the industry formed regional councils and started pushing the issue in recent years. The security side of the industry now realizes that it takes the effort from transportation and logistics companies and their insurance carriers to bring the issue into light and make law enforcement, the public, and other segments of the industry aware of the problem.

When I joined the industry side of the equation in 1997, several regional industry councils and a fairly active national group known as the National Cargo Security Council (NCSC) existed. The Eastern Regional Council was active in New York and New Jersey and cargo associations existed in northern and southern California. These groups advocated for the industry in their own ways and under their own bylaws. The sharing of theft information through company security managers, although a good model, left a lot to be desired. Information sharing should have been taken beyond the industry security management groups and associations. Even though transportation companies compete for the same business in many cases, the sharing of nonproprietary information related to theft methods and security risks made perfect sense.

The director of security at my company was Tom Sheets. He was involved in the NCSC and was an active advocate for regional council formation, information sharing, and networking between industry security management and law enforcement. I attended several NCSC functions and started to understand the need to support the industry by building awareness and sharing information. It also became apparent that building law enforcement contacts with officers who handled cargo and commercial vehicle thefts was extremely important to the industry. As a regional security manager for a multimode transportation entity, having reliable contacts throughout a region was vital. My jurisdiction included five states and a foreign country. It appeared that the best way to build useful contacts was to start a council in our region.

I started contacting several people from other companies and proposed a meeting. Five people attended our organizational meeting: Ray Rios of SAIA Trucking, Jaime Olivarez of Central (now with Yellow), Charles Bergeron of AF (now with FedEx), Nolan Burns of Watkins (now with FedEx) and me. We decided to form the Southwest Transportation Security Council (SWTSC). Our goals were to: (1) start an industry council, (2) build a law enforcement network, and (3) provide educational opportunities for law enforcement about the inner workings of the industry.

As a fledgling organization, we did not try to formalize our existence immediately and we slowly started building the group via monthly meetings and reaching out to the local and state police contacts who worked on commercial vehicle thefts. Distribution lists were built and a small communication network was started. We achieved some local success in assisting law enforcement to find complainants and investigating related offenses and thus started to build credibility with law enforcement. We devised a half-day training seminar for law enforcement agencies to explain how the transportation industry operates and how the paperwork flows. The training also spoke to the mission of the council and our desire to build a private–public partnership. Little by little, more members joined the council and our distribution list grew. We started transmitting information about stolen loads to both industry members and law enforcement agencies via e-mail. An FBI agent from the local major theft unit participated and began keeping the records of the incidents. That lasted until September 11, 2001 when the terrorist attacks in New York and Washington took away our FBI agent participation.

Around that time, the FBI agent introduced me to Millie DeAnda of the North Texas Crime Commission (NTCC). When she saw what we were trying to accomplish, she invited our council to become a committee of the commission and she offered administrative assistance in return for providing law enforcement training related to cargo theft and other cargo crimes.

This arrangement worked for many years as the SWTSC membership and law enforcement contact network continued to grow. The council expanded its communication network and sent BOLO alerts to a much wider audience. It sponsored and organized two law enforcement training seminars a year and started sending and receiving information from other councils and associations. The council also developed law enforcement training covering cargo theft and drug shipment interdiction in commercial vehicle lanes.

The SWTSC was eventually able to train law enforcement officers who specialized in cargo crime investigation and provide scholarships to the Miami Dade TOMCATS Cargo Theft School in Florida and other training opportunities. In 2006, the council began looking for a way to archive the BOLO alert information so that it could be stored and retrieved. The Supply Chain Information Sharing and Analysis Center offered to put the information in its database and further share it with industry and law enforcement agencies.

With the addition of the database piece, the ability to collect and analyze cargo theft data began. The information, as seen in the first chapter, keeps maturing and allows us to further understand the risks and threats. The analysis also identifies changes that the perpetrators make in response to industry and law enforcement actions. As the capabilities of the council enhanced, it continued growing in size and influence. More and more successes were seen with the BOLO alert system and in the ability to connect the dots by industry and law enforcement. When law enforcement is in need of assistance such as bait freight, equipment, an undercover warehouse, or to identify a complainant, a request to the industry council membership usually fills the need.

As the council continued to grow, the relationship with the North Texas Crime Commission became too cumbersome for processing payments and other administrative functions. In 2010, the SWTSC applied for and received its own designation as a nonprofit 501(c) 6 organization. This step allowed it to control its own financial operations. The council's sole income had been company member dues that enabled us to provide law enforcement training events, scholarships for other industry training activities, and appreciation events for our law enforcement partners. We have also been able to purchase equipment for their use in cargo investigations.

SWSTC advocated for a cargo task force in Texas because the state is continually identified as a hot spot for this type of criminal activity. We were not completely successful but because we were able to provide ample information on the issue, District One of the Texas State Police named cargo theft as a priority for its investigative agents. This has really helped the industry in North Texas and, because of those contacts, it is easier to get police involvement when incidents occur elsewhere in the state. The larger cities in Texas have dedicated detectives who work these crimes and industries interact often with them. Having these resources yields smoother investigation and communication between public and private entities.

Industry Security Councils

In 1999, when we started this group, one of our first goals was to improve the communicaiton between law enforcement agencies in North Texas. The Dallas–Fort Worth Metropolitan area includes 28 police jurisdictions. The growth of SWTSC into a large group with reach to industry groups and law enforcement agencies all around the United States is amazing, something I never envisioned. In today's computerized world, building a network like this is not hard; it just takes time, effort, and continuous networking and relationship building.

We eventually started sending communications to the other councils and several of them started participating fully in the BOLO alert communication system, most notably the Eastern Region Cargo Theft Association and the Southeast Cargo Security Council. Sending information to other councils results in sharing it with various police agencies and freight-related companies. The insurance industry-backed Verisk Cargo-Net recently joined in the sending of BOLO alerts. It also maintains a database and obtains information from public-sector groups through the Insurance Services Organization program that other industry sources cannot access. This relationship further enhanced the industry's communication reach and it should grow further in the future.

Each council determines its own membership rules, activities, and dues. When the SWTSC was formed, we made a distinct effort not to be a secret society and planned to allow all entities in the supply chain to become members. We included vendors as long as they did not use the information to "chase ambulances" and understood the council mission. Allowing the insurance industry investigators into the fold has really enhanced information sharing and the identification of theft patterns and problems. By extending our membership to relevant parties, we have been able to promote the information sharing and increase the understanding of security risks and

Here is an example of how the council has grown and how its reach has grown much further than we ever anticipated when we started the group. I participated in a conference call with a private investigator who is a member of the council and a Nebraska State Police criminal investigative division captain. The call concerned fictitious pick-ups of brokered loads at meat plants in Nebraska, Kansas, Oklahoma, and Northern Texas. Prior to the call, I contacted the SC-ISAC and other organizations to gather information concerning this ongoing type of theft. Because it is fairly prevalent in the Texas Panhandle, Kansas, and Nebraska, I was able to provide the Nebraska group with information and a report from another member of the SWTSC who had already been investigating these issues. The call was very productive and was a good first step toward working up a strategy to deal with the problem by the public sector.

About an hour later, another member of the council who performs security investigations for a brokerage group called me. He was looking for a contact in Omaha, Nebraska, because his group had assigned a load to a carrier that they now realized he was using a false identity. I was able to immediately connect him with a law enforcement contact who already knew of the issue so that appropriate action could be taken. An arrest was made and the follow-up investigation will go well beyond this offense. The targeted load was also prevented from being stolen.

threats in the transportation industry. Because the council is at the forefront, we can make other public officials aware of industry issues. Hiding the information in a closet does not do anyone any good. Sharing nonsensitive information about stolen product, methods used, vehicle descriptions, and other data may aid recovery. Since the council's archived information started maturing, we have been able to find complainants for cases and achieve property recovery long after thefts have taken place. Information sharing is a win–win for public agencies and private industry.

Southwest Transportation Security Council

The Southwest Transportation Security Council (SWTSC) is based in Dallas, Texas. Meetings are held monthly and hosted at member facilities. Local police investigators are invited to the meetings to discuss local and regional issues. The council website is www.swtsc.com and contact numbers and further information are made available at meetings. Any company operating in the supply chain in the Southwest should consider participating in this group. The information and benefits received far outweigh the costs of the association dues. The benefits include access to a large law enforcement contact list, a wide variety of industry contacts, and many sources and resources for services.

The council also provides the BOLO alert system that can transmit loss information to appropriate parties throughout the country quickly. The system also gives members access to alerts from other regions to keep the industry aware of the ongoing cargo theft activity. This participation in information sharing and networking keeps participants up to date via contacts with industry members and law enforcement agencies. Membership also provides access to cargo security training events, important conferences, and industry and law enforcement networking.

Eastern Region Cargo Theft Association

I believe that the Eastern Region Cargo Theft Association (ERCTA), which is based in New York and New Jersey, is the oldest council of its type and was the first one I encountered.

I was introduced by Murry Cohen, a company colleague who was an association member long before his retirement. This was my first exposure to the concept of a regional industry council that brought industry security management together with law enforcement. Its current Chairman is Kurt Duesderdick who works for National Retail Systems. The Eastern Region is very viable and has been a great partner in the flow of BOLO alerts and other communications. Their membership is robust and the network of law enforcement contacts for their region is vigorous.

ERCTA really understands the concept of public–private cooperation, particularly with information sharing. It also furnishes scholarships to allow law enforcement to attend training events and works closely with the New Jersey State Police Cargo Task Force. For companies operating in this region, membership in this group and access to its information and law enforcement network is tremendously valuable. At the time of this writing, no website was listed for the group.

Western States Cargo Theft Association

The Western States Cargo Theft Association (WSCTA) has northern and southern chapters. The southern group is based in the Los Angeles area while the northern operates from the San Francisco Bay area. This association has been in existence a long time also. It holds monthly meetings at member facilities but its membership remains a little more restrictive. It is not fully committed to the BOLO alert program but has shared some information. The association maintains a very good relationship with law enforcement authorities including the California Highway Patrol Cargo Theft Interdiction Program task force that focuses on cargo crime in California. The WSCTA website at http://www.wscta.com/ provides contact and membership information.

Mid-South Cargo Security Council

The Mid-South Cargo Security Council is based in Memphis, Tennessee, and has supported the public–private partnership in its region for many years. Unlike other regional councils, the Mid-South does not participate in the BOLO system but does maintain a close relationship with the Memphis Cargo Task Force and relevant law enforcement agencies. The council is very active and provides great benefits and information for industry members operating in the region. The council meets monthly and provides activities for industry members and law enforcement groups including training events and conferences. Its website is http://midsouthcsc.org/.

Southeast Transportation Security Council

The Southeast Transportation Security Council (SETSC) was started a few years after the Southwest group and is based in the Atlanta, Georgia, area. It is an effective organization that partners with the Georgia Bureau of Investigation and State Police. Before his retirement, one of its leaders was a Department of Agriculture Investigator so that agency was very actively involved. SETSC is a very active group that conducts monthly meetings and participates in the BOLO system to share information with other councils. Georgia has always been an active area for cargo theft, especially around Atlanta and its border with Florida puts the state right at the gateway of cargo theft traffic moving south. The SETSC website (at http://www.setsc.org/) contains information about membership and events.

Mid-West Cargo Security Council

This council has not been very active and needs better industry participation. It currently has one of the best law enforcement task forces sponsored by the Illinois State Police and the

National Insurance Crime Bureau (NICB) is based in the region. The council has the pieces in place to become more effective. It does not meet monthly, has no website, and does not participate in the BOLO system. The SWTSC has compiled distribution lists for law enforcement and industry in this part of the country to fill the lack of communication and information sharing. One of the best yearly training events is held by the Illinois State Police Mid-West Cargo Task and is well attended. The Mid-West needs to promote public–private partnership because cargo crime activity including splinter group operations in the area continues to increase.

Virginia–Carolinas Cargo Security Council

The VCCSC is the newest regional council and combines a very interested private industry team and involved law enforcement groups. Thanks to recent NICB meetings focusing on cargo theft in the Carolinas, awareness has been raised. These states now have the interest and tools to maintain a very good organization and participate in the communication and networking activities of other councils. The Southern Police Institute hosted cargo theft law enforcement training and even requested the VCCSC to present the concept and discuss its public–private partnership. Its website, at http://www.vccsc.org/, provides contact and other information. We look forward to having this new group in the brotherhood of councils to share information and promote law enforcement networking. The SWTSC developed and maintained contacts in this region through a distribution list, but the formation of a regional council will enhance the communication and law enforcement networking exponentially.

Pharmaceutical Cargo Security Coalition

This council is a bit different from the others but was born from the same need. Pharmaceuticals represented some of the biggest targets of organized thieves both in transit and in storage in the supply chain. As pharmaceutical shippers joined transportation security councils after suffering in-transit losses, they saw the value of starting a group specific to their industry and issues. When Chuck Forsaith of Perdue Pharma started the Pharmaceutical Cargo Security Coalition (PSCS), he followed suit with the cargo councils and became involved in information sharing and education, both for industry and law enforcement. The coalition became very successful in a short time and is now a significant partner in the cargo theft communication system. The PSCS website is accessible at http://www.pcscpharma.com/ and contacts and membership information are available online. Pharmaceutical products at one time ranked at the top of the product break-down chart reviewed in Chapter 1. Based on this coalition and industry promotion of communication and information sharing, thefts of these products have significantly reduced.

These councils and associations have proven immensely valuable. The SWTSC recently teamed with the Texas Department of Public Safety, the National Insurance Crime Bureau, and Hewlett Packard to host a two-day Texas Cargo Summit for industry and law enforcement. The event is free and all participants receive lunch, registration packets, educational materials, and training that will be certified for law enforcement participants. Within two weeks of announcing the summit event, the limit of 235 attendees was reached. This shows the great interest from both sides of the public–private sector in the issue.

These training seminars and networking events are very valuable to the freight industry and law enforcement groups. I do not know of another industry that works together as well as this one does, thanks to the councils and the people who participate and support them. I learn something new each day I work in this industry and I appreciate the education and support I receive from all the participants on both sides of the equation. Who ever thought that moving a box, pallet, or truckload from point A to Point B could be this complex?

The councils filled a large void by creating a far-reaching communication system that provides both information and assistance. Police are the last line of defense; they are not recovery plans. It is important for a cargo operation to have written security and recovery plans in place long before they suffer major losses. Prevention, planning, and understanding the risks go a long way in protecting shipments. If you have to call the police to recover losses, your procedures and processes have failed. Knowing whom to call, networking, and making contacts will make the response quicker and more focused, but you really never want to get to this point. By involvement in councils and their communication systems, you will gain awareness of the theft problem, understand the current risks, and have access to resources to assist you in building an efficient and effective cargo security program. As a transportation security manager, membership in these organizations gives you an unequaled force multiplier at your fingertips.

National Transportation Security Organizations

When I first entered the industry in 1997, The National Cargo Security Council was the preeminent organization for security managers and providers. I do not know the history of the organization but it was well regarded and very active. Within a few years, the organization changed its name to the International Cargo Security Council (ICSC) and attempted to extend its reach and influence. That move started the downward spiral of the group until it became extinct in about 2006. It would not be fair for me to provide a postmortem as I really do not know enough of the facts to intelligently discuss the failure that left a large void for a national organization focused on freight transportation security.

Several groups have stepped in to provide some oversight on the national level. Those groups include the Supply Chain Security and Loss Prevention Council (SCSLPC) of the American Trucking Association (ATA), the National Insurance Crime Bureau, and the American Society of Industrialized Security (ASIS) Supply Chain Security Council. These groups are not trying to replace the ICSC/NCSC and their agendas are not the same. The ATA-SCSLPC is a committee of the ATA with a focus on the trucking side of the equation. Trucking is the largest piece of the pie and we all understand the involvement of trucking in all of the modes of freight transportation. The ATA-SCSLPC website contains the following statement about its mission:

> The ATA Supply Chain Security and Loss Prevention Council is the only national organization dedicated exclusively to addressing, establishing and advancing those policies and practices that achieve maximum security (supply chain personnel, cargo, truck, facility, information and the homeland); effective risk management and loss control, cargo theft reduction, successful claims management; and secure, nonviolent work environments. It exists to serve, promote and create value for members and the industry through research, education, information dissemination, peer and law enforcement interaction, consensus building and incentive programs which inspire corporate and individual excellence and contribute to a more secure and profitable trucking industry and nation.

As someone who has worked with the ATA-SCSLPC and attended and provided instruction at its conferences, I know the organization provides great value to its membership. However, its membership requirements and fees are different from those of the former NCSC and it does not serve the same set of entities. The ATA-SCSLPC conducts a yearly conference and works closely within the ATA to provide its service and guidance related to supply chain security to its members. The ATA-SCSLPC has not become an active part of the BOLO system run by the councils.

National Insurance Crime Bureau

The NICB has really stepped up its involvement in cargo theft in recent years and has become a driving force behind the National Cargo Theft Task Force. The national bureau is involved through its agents who sit on regional cargo theft councils and by sponsoring and supporting theft-related training events around the country.

The NICB originally adopted a National Commercial Vehicle and Cargo Theft Prevention Initiative in February 17, 2005 and revised and readopted it on October 20, 2010. The initiative was a call for the adoption of a nationwide initiative by the federal government, in cooperation with private industry and state and local governments to combat cargo theft. The national strategy involved a task force structure and funding for and creation of new cargo theft task forces in several key states. The eight-point strategy included increasing the number task forces, providing funding, increasing cargo theft penalties, and making the public aware of the dangers to public health arising from thefts of consumable goods. A critical component of the strategy was the need for intelligence gathering and information sharing and public awareness. The NICB also formed several task force subcommittees specializing in best practices, government affairs, technology, and public awareness. The subcommittees compile and develop information in their areas for use by the task force. Interested individuals can access https://www.nationalcargothefttaskforce.org/ncttf/start. action and become contacts.

NICB has been very supportive to the transportation industry and its contacts and influence have aided efforts to solve cargo theft problems. However, NICB is not a voluntary organization like the ICSC. It is a totally different entity involved in a much different way.

Some associations represent segments of the supply chain but at present no voluntary global organization exists solely to advocate for freight transportation security related to cargo theft issues. Is this a void that needs to be filled? The regional councils do a good job of covering their regions and providing a national reach via the BOLO communication system. They interact for training and other cross functions. What is in place now seems to work and is continuing to grow and handle frequent requests to be added to the distribution lists.

I guess the question is whether we have a need for a national council or association? I believe a need may exist but a national group would have to be organized to coexist and function with the current regional council configurations. Cargo theft is a national issue, and the National Cargo Theft Task Force (NCTTF) initiative is a good start. The NCTTF could be the basis of a national organization if it allowed more interaction. Cargo theft is a regional concern. A company that suffers a cargo theft in a certain location needs assistance in that area immediately. Acquiring valuable contacts through regional councils provides the best assistance in those situations. These national and regional groups should work as partners to benefit all segments of society except cargo thieves.

ASIS Supply Chain and Transportation Security Council

This council is a committee of the large international ASIS organization. ASIS is the largest and most comprehensive security organization in the world and has committees for just about every infrastructure. The SCTSC works across all modes of freight transportation and its committees have expertise in most areas of supply chains and transportation including maritime, aviation, ground transport, railroad, and supply chain security. Every committee is responsible for generating white papers and webinars and submitting relevant works for annual seminars.

The SCTSC council members attend local chapter meetings to update chapters on council activities. Its web page, http://www.asisonline.org/councils/TRAN.xml, posts articles and event information. SCTSC members are available to comment on news related to supply chain security as subject matter experts. At the ASIS annual conference, the SCTSC maintains a booth to provide information from council resources and also conducts training and round table discussions.

ASIS has opportunities for council members to serve on various committees (for example, rail, trucking, or maritime shipping) that relate to the SCTSC. Even though the ASIS councils do not participate in information sharing or the BOLO system, many of the council and committee members belong to regional councils and they cross-pollinate through dual memberships. The ASIS councils are more about processes, procedures, and best practices. They act as good sources of ideas and resources but are not concerned with day-to-day communications handled by the regional industry councils. The networking provided by ASIS membership and participation reaches across the entire supply chain.

Transported Asset Protection Association (TAPA)

TAPA was founded in 1997 to prevent warehouse thefts and enhance facility security. It provides guidelines for distribution facilities through Freight Security Requirements (FSRs) and developed an auditing process with a certification standard. Around 2005, TAPA moved to issue guidelines for in-transit moves by establishing Trucking Security Requirements (TSRs) and implemented an auditing process for the TSRs in 2010.

My observation of the technology members involved with TAPA indicated that they were acrimonious toward trucking carriers and transportation because most of the group did not work or operate in that space and lacked an understanding of its value. Many times what they required or wanted was way over the premium they were willing to pay for the service and even unrealistic. However, time, maturity, and experience made the organization far more reality based and cooperative.

The FSRs and TSRs it issued make sense, are reasonable, and serve as realistic guidelines for carriers and service providers.

Security is not always about spending money; it often simply requires working smarter. TAPA is now accepted into the mainstream of supply chain security since it moderated its views and started accepting membership outside the technology world. Information about TAPA can be found at http://www.tapaonline.org/. If you are tasked with building a security plan, the TAPA FSRs and TSRs are very good starting points for devising guidelines and requirements.

Information Sharing

The most important part of networking and group involvement is the sharing of information. Companies that have similar interests and operations can assist each other in nonproprietary ways by sharing information related to risks and threats that face the entire industry including manufacturers, shippers, carriers in all modes, insurers, transportation security vendors, security service providers, and all entities with interests in protecting the supply chain. When some or all of these people gather in the same room, they can all relate experiences or incidents that will allow others to learn new tactics. Sharing information is a way of not having to reinvent the wheel, learning from experts, and hearing about risks and threats that may arise in the future. It is also a great way to learn about effective products and efficient resources for all types of security problems. Discussions about losses and recoveries, where they occurred, what was taken, where equipment was recovered, and evidence at the scene paint a very informative picture. Having knowledge about these incidents allows you and your company a much better chance of recovery if a theft occurs.

When we first started talking about sharing information on a much more public scale to raise awareness and analyze the issues, many industry insiders feared such activity. They were afraid that being open about losses would place the industry in the wrong light or worried that their companies would lose business or suffer other consequences. This has just not been the case.

A few holdouts continue to guard their information. They are only hurting their own companies and hindering better security and recovery operations. One security director of a company was adamant about not sharing information when his company suffered a loss of a cargo of flat screen televisions. He refused to share the details of the theft or the location where the recovery took place—in this case, a west Texas city. About six weeks later, his company was hit again at the same location. A vendor of the shipping company reached out to the SWTSC after the shipper had trouble getting an investigative law enforcement response. A call was made to state police in the area. The investigator was aware of the previous offense and knew where the empty trailer was dropped after the earlier incident. Quite a bit of time had passed. When he went to the known location, he found the abandoned empty trailer from the latest offense. Had the victimized company been involved in information sharing and communication network and immediately revealed the information, law enforcement would have had an opportunity to place the recovery location under surveillance before the unit was abandoned.

Sharing information does not require a company to reveal names or proprietary information. It simply means a company can get the necessary information out in the quickest manner to the most authorized persons to help it recover its property. Another benefit is entering product information into the archived systems. If it is found later, it can be returned to the correct party. All of this makes perfect sense.

A good case in point about sharing information and under-standing how thieves operate involved a load of stolen baby formula in Michigan. The company that sustained the loss was aware of the thieves' MO and informed the responding law enforcement. Based on the information provided by the complainant, the police were able to focus their search within miles of the loss where they found the stolen tractor and arrested a suspect leaving the recovery location. Then they focused their search based on the company investigator's information and found the trailer a few miles away, where the other suspects were painting over trailer logos. By understanding the latest activities of the thieves, the company recovered its load.

Without studying past cases and understanding current cargo crime activity, you place yourself in a position of not knowing a criminal's current MO, leaving you unable to advise the police. Remember, few police officers responding to these calls have any idea about the methods of the criminals. It is really up to security personnel to understand the incident, direct the information to law enforcement, or utilize networking contacts to contact a law enforcement officer specializing in cargo theft in the jurisdiction where the crime occurred. The small number of cargo theft task forces in the United States means that a company probably has limited choices but it may be able to find a commercial vehicle theft investigator or state police vehicle enforcement officer who has some knowledge of such crimes from participating in cargo theft information sharing.

The more that look, the more ears that listen, and the more persons who understand cargo crime makes for a force multiplier beyond your security team and one agency that responds to make a report. The National Crime Information Computer (NCIC) was set up to allow police to enter information about vehicle registrations, vehicle identification numbers, and other data. It is a very good system for confirmation but not for broadcast capability. Why would you not use all the resources available to have the best chance to make a recovery?

Archiving and Analysis

The first step was sharing information obtained from the councils with their law enforcement partners and members. During the early days of the BOLO alert system, no single database captured relevant data and that meant no data were analyzed. I often received calls from members during the early stages of information sharing. They asked whether I remembered a certain incident or report on a certain stolen commodity. The only way of checking then was looking back through e-mails or reviewing a personal file containing alerts. We found some information but we were not always successful. We knew we needed a database where we could store reports; enter important data from incidents into predetermined spreadsheet sections; and capture commodity, value, and recovery information to aid efforts to identify cargo theft adversaries.

The SWTSC found just such a partner in the Supply Chain Information Sharing and Analysis Center (SC-ISAC). In 2006, SWTSC started entering information on every cargo theft incident reported. While quite a bit of information concerned certain cargo theft groups, no one had ever really taken a close look. After archiving started, sharing expanded and industry people started to understand the goals of the councils and the ISAC. As the amount of data grew and matured, supply chain operators started to obtain very clear pictures of theft incidents.

Almost everyone in the industry who worked with FTL shipments was aware of the influence of ethnic crews from South Florida. Most insiders had good ideas of their activities, targets, and methods. Industry and law enforcement had some facts but did not have the capability of studying large numbers of offenses through the United States.

Even as this database was put in place, many involved agencies and companies refused to share information. Companies did not understand the dynamics of information sharing and police agencies long believed that all crime information had to be shrouded in secrecy. In retrospect, we now know that shining a light on the nonsensitive information is a much better policy and most agencies now understand that not all information surrounding an offense is sensitive. Over time, law enforcement agents and agencies found that sharing even scaled-down batch data was helpful to all concerned parties.

Expanding the number of data sources progressed in baby steps but many groups now continue to press the issue and lead the way. In 2007, I left my transportation security industry position and joined LoJack Supply Chain Integrity as its director of law enforcement services. My duties included recruiting law enforcement members for the SC-ISAC and expanding information sharing. This was a very good fit because I knew what benefits would result from sharing information generated by industry councils. This intelligence is vital for developing sufficient understanding of the threats and risks of industry thefts. My position allowed me to work with both the law enforcement sector and private industry. Understanding both sides of public–private operations made it easy for me to liaison with both sides. Through the SC-ISAC and the SWTSC, I pursued law enforcement contacts, completed relevant law enforcement and industry training and "preached the gospel" of cargo theft risks to any group that showed interest.

The SC-ISAC data matured and allowed us to confirm changes in activities of criminals in response to industry and law enforcements actions and reactions. The ability to provide definitive data to industry and law enforcement and discuss it intelligently and passionately effected changes. A case in point was the introduction of an SWTSC cargo theft template form provided by the Texas Department of Public Safety. The District 1 state police agreed to send theft information directly to its road units if the information was placed in its template. The template, which found its way around the country, seems to serve as the reporting form of choice.

These are small victories but they build credibility with both industry entities and law enforcement authorities. By compiling and submitting data to law enforcement, building distribution lists, and networking with various agencies, I have been able to train and work with many state police agencies and build great relationships that ultimately produce quick assistance with recovery efforts by members of the industry.

The archived information in the database brings more successes every day. We see more property identified and connected to specific offenses. The identification of more crime trends and patterns leads to more credibility with police agencies. After an industry organization starts providing assistance, for example, in finding complainants or identifying carrier equipment, the public sector starts to understand the benefits of partnerships with industry. Great benefits have resulted from information sharing, analyzing data, and working in partnership. Any company not participating in industry programs is not using all the tools available to transportation security professionals.

Conclusion

In the past five years, two hard-hit groups that made the most of information sharing and analysis and improved supply chain security are the tobacco and pharmaceutical shippers. The tobacco industry really was the first to make major changes, demand accountability, and use technology to improve the visibility of their shipments from origin to destination. The industry also began participating in national and regional groups to build network assets and obtain resources to protect their products in transit and in warehouses. Tobacco loads were hit often. A tobacco load is worth millions of dollars and generates huge amounts of taxes. FTL thefts were common until the industry took action. All industries must take steps to thwart crime; if the police must be called, a company's plans and procedures have failed. Tobacco companies built security programs that included driver awareness programs, installation of covert tracking technology and the use of the carrier evaluation matrix. When we look at best practices later in its book, you will understand the value of a layered security approach for theft prevention.

The pharmaceutical industry took a different approach and started its own council. The industry has been very successful in lowering losses and promoting the use of security resources and tools that give their carriers better chances to succeed. We still see some pharmaceutical losses but they are far smaller than they once were. Tobacco and pharmaceuticals always ranked at the tops of product theft charts (see Chapter 1). Since they expanded their security efforts, they are no longer at the tops of stolen commodity charts. This does not mean they are not targets; it simply means that criminals know that certain companies have taken steps to make stealing from them much more difficult. A recent stolen load of cigarettes contained a covert tracking device. It took the covert tracking company for which I work only 42 minutes to make full recovery with no loss of integrity.

Taking action can make a difference. Many companies view security as a necessary evil instead of an activity that can positively affect the bottom line. The prevention of one major cargo theft will pay for security efforts for a pretty good while. Targeted industries should look at these examples and take some of the same steps. They should share information and use it to build effective security and recovery plans. Unfortunately, several companies that have been victimized many times have not made any significant changes to their operations to prevent further problems. The cargo criminals know who these companies are. It is pleasing to watch security professionals who have taken the time to understand cargo theft issues and provide real security solutions and options to their employers to achieve continued loss reduction.

Chapter 5

Law Enforcement Responses

Introduction

The overall law enforcement response to cargo thefts in most circumstances has been underwhelming for many reasons. Obviously, unsatisfactory response is not the case in every jurisdiction because some task forces actively react to and investigate such crimes. Some of the problem relates to crime-reporting issues. Most states do not have specific statutes covering cargo theft and adjudication can vary depending on how a crime is reported. If cargo is stolen along with a tractor and trailer, the incident is treated as a commercial vehicle theft offense and the cargo in the trailer is a supplement to the vehicle crime. When a tractor and trailer are recovered, cargo becomes an afterthought. Vehicle detectives are not always trained to deal with issues beyond the vehicles and may not understand the cargo losses involved in the equation.

Some departments actually cover cargo crime through their auto theft units but these are more exceptions than rules. Therefore, when police crime statistics and records do not include cargo theft data, the agencies cannot be expected to form task forces unless they see good reasons. We all understand that reality. For many years, the Dallas Police Department employed one auto theft detective, David Wallace, who also had cargo theft responsibility. This is a city of over a million people that constitutes a problem area for cargo crime. From an industry standpoint, a single detective was better than nothing. Over time, the SWTSC was able to lobby the Dallas department to at least assign cargo, commercial vehicle, and trailer thefts to the Auto Theft Section so that they were assigned to one detective. Before that improvement was made, trailer thefts were assigned to various burglary and theft units at the precinct level and coordination of enforcement and investigation efforts was nonexistent.

Detective Wallace soon became acquainted with the industry by attending SWTSC meetings and training. He understood the scenarios and criminals and became a very good source and resource for area cargo theft information. A task force or assigned detectives can make a huge difference in crime investigation. When a detective or group of detectives work certain crimes—drugs, robberies, burglaries, or cargo thefts—they start to understand the crime, the criminals, and all the other moving parts. Stolen property must be disposed of so police investigators identify fencing operations, pawn shops, and online sources that deal in stolen goods. When suspects are identified or arrested, specialized investigators conduct interviews and build local, regional, and even national intelligence. Because cargo theft information has been compiled, officers have a great deal of background, resources, and sources to assist them in solving crimes and recovering stolen property. If an area does not have a task force or at least one assigned cargo theft detective, its ability to investigate crimes and recover stolen property is greatly hampered by the lack of organization and information.

Information is the big difference between the haves and the have-nots. Cargo thefts frequently victimize the have-nots.

As I was writing this section of the book, I received an e-mail from a member needing a law enforcement contact in Phoenix, Arizona. The area lacks a task force but I was able to provide the member with contacts at the Phoenix Police Department and the state police. Both contacts have participated in information distribution for years and I know they will assist our member based on their association with our council and its relationship with their state and national chapters of the International Association of Auto Theft Investigators (IAATI). Through LoJack SCI's relationship with IAATI, we have been able to help bring cargo theft awareness to IAATI through training and networking with its national and regional chapters. This organization is a natural partner for the freight industry organizations and companies.

This is where the industry councils, information sharing, and awareness of the issues by industry security management can assist law enforcement investigators in jurisdictions of the have-nots and also put them in touch with the closest state police or task force groups that have valuable information. Actually several of the have-nots became interested in crime data, participated in distribution of information, and are becoming more knowledgeable about cargo crime and many detectives, through their own motivation and interest, have become reliable contacts and work hard on their cases.

Cargo Theft Law Enforcement Responses

Cargo theft is the poster child for federal law enforcement action. Stolen cargo is almost always moved from the jurisdiction where the act occurred to another city, county, or state. By the time the agency making the original police report obtains all the necessary information and enters it into the National Crime Information Computer (NCIC), the stolen goods are already many miles away. Although federal agencies are involved in some of the task forces, they seldom actively assist in investigations or pursue prosecutions to the federal level. This lack of action by federal law enforcement agencies does not appear to be headed for change. The void must therefore be filled by the industry councils and organizations that build relationships with state police and local investigators in the areas where the most cargo crime occurs. Several federal investigators from the Food & Drug Administration and Department of Agriculture have done great work in several locales.

The existing cargo theft task forces have done some very good work and provide much information and partnership benefits to industry security and operations managers. As I was writing this book, I received an e-mail message from the commander of the Miami Dade Police Department TOMCATS unit advising that due to budgetary constraints, the TOMCATS were going to be disbanded. The message did not explain how cargo theft cases were going to be handled in the future or provide contact information for follow-up. The TOMCATS have been the primary cargo theft task force for many years. Many former TOMCATS investigators found their way into the industry and they have been the cornerstones of investigations and intelligence gathering about Florida cargo theft crews for many years.

The TOMCATS hosted a yearly training seminar that became almost mandatory for law enforcement and industry investigators. This disbanding is a huge blow to cargo theft law enforcement efforts and will aid the thieves to continue to victimize the industry and commit crimes with less pressure. It is too early to tell what will happen, but the elimination of the TOMCATS is not welcome news for an industry that already has insufficient task forces and law enforcement contacts.

The TOMCATS task force enjoyed federal involvement and participation. Although most of the investigations and investigators were local, federal support gave them funding and overcame jurisdictional issues. It also made them very effective. Remember, property stolen in another jurisdiction and transported to Miami does not fall under the investigation responsibilities of the Miami Dade Police Department. When freight is identified as stolen, a complainant can be identified, and a police agency report can be found for the property, the police in the jurisdiction where the property is found can react. As a result of eliminating the TOMCATS program, all of the intelligence and investigative work aided by informants will slowly dwindle away. When Miami has no unit to maintain intelligence, informants, and underground contacts, the chances of recovery in that area will greatly decrease and play directly into the hands of cargo theft crews.

The TOMCATS consisted of eight Miami Dade Police Department (MDPD) personnel including a lieutenant, a sergeant, a Florida Highway Patrol representative, and a Florida DOT investigator. The group also had a counterpart FBI Supervisor and five FBI agents assigned to the unit according to the last update received from the group supervisor before the disband memo arrived.

Recovery of stolen cargo has always been unpredictable at best. When the South Florida crews pulled heists several years ago, most of the equipment and cargo came directly south from theft locations. A company and law enforcement had about a 16-hour window in which to recover the stolen freight before it found its way into temporary storage for a short time before being moved again. Because the MO changed somewhat from the earlier days and the criminals now change tractors closer to crime scenes and stash trailers to conduct counter-surveillance to determine whether cargo-imbedded GPS is involved, pursuers may have a little more time to effect recovery but time is still of the essence.

One task the SWTSC has been trying to accomplish with its distribution lists is adding state police interdiction squads. These squads are on the road most of the time and transmitting theft information to them can be a huge force multiplier in the first stages of a search. Interdiction squads are great resources for pursuing stolen units. Also keying commercial vehicle enforcement officers into these crimes and methods of operation will give them more information about what factors they should look for during their inspections and stops. The state police interdiction squads that work the north–south freeways on the east coast from New York to Miami need to be on some council distribution list. They should receive BOLO alerts and communications because they are in prime positions to find stolen units or aid recovery if a unit has GPS tracking equipment.

Several cargo theft task forces exist around the country. In Florida, the highway patrol still offers a Statewide Cargo Theft Task Force. This group has done a lot of good work over the years through the state and is still available to contact. Florida also still has the Marion County Sheriff's Office Task Force. Ed Dean, the sheriff, has been a driving force in the National Cargo Theft Task Force and the push for a national strategy.

In California, several units have some cargo theft responsibilities. They include the Los Angeles County Sheriff's Office CARGOCATS, the California Highway Patrol Cargo Theft Interdiction Program (CTIP) that utilizes several units around the state from the Mexican border to the Bay area. California also has the Los Angeles Police Department's BADCATS and its Airport Crimes Unit. San Francisco International Airport has AIRCATS. As shown in the charts in Chapter 1, California is almost always the top location for cargo theft crimes and the state has positioned law enforcement groups to assist. These units are highly effective and they have the information, intelligence, and expertise to succeed. The CTIP group keeps statistics and records that assist with recoveries and also shares batch data with the SC-ISAC.

The Georgia Cargo Theft Task Force is run by the Georgia Bureau of Investigation and it started operation in 2008. The task force has been very successful in making recoveries and taking down some very large fencing operations and has a great partnership with the Southeast Cargo Security Council. The two entities helped establish the Georgia Cargo Theft Alert System (https://www.gacargotheft.com/).

The Illinois State Police Midwest Cargo Theft Task Force has worked hand in hand with private-sector counterparts on the Midwest Cargo Security Council and also with the SWTSC, the Eastern Region CTA, and the National Insurance Crime Bureau. During its short existence, it moved fast by hosting several highly attended training conferences and becoming a resource in an area of the country where it was sorely needed.

In Kentucky, the Louisville Metropolitan Police Department and the state police have dedicated cargo investigative groups that have been great resources and lately faced South Florida crews operating in and around Louisville. These crews, when they move into new regions, continue to use the same methods of operation but start from a different base. The Louisville crews have been very active in the midwest recently.

The New Jersey State Police (NJSP) have a dedicated cargo theft task force that has been extremely busy. Cargo theft analysis shows a great deal of empty stolen midwest equipment found in New Jersey. The state police have identified and arrested quite a few South Florida crew members involved in thefts or receiving stolen property in their area. The group also has a splendid relationship with the Eastern Region Cargo Theft Association. Their private–public partnership is a model. Lieutenant Mike McDonnell is retiring. He will be missed by the industry but we are sure the NJSP group will continue his excellent work. The Eastern Region Chairman, Kurt Duesderdick, made it easy for the two groups to work together. The NJSP shares batch data with industry sources and works with other law enforcement agencies and insurance investigators.

The Nevada Viper Auto and Cargo Task Force in Las Vegas is a good resource for the industry. Most crime in Las Vegas involves the stealing of dropped trailers or unattended rigs from casino and hotel parking lots.

The Pennsylvania State Police lacks a designated cargo task force but a number of its troop sergeants are industry contacts who assist the industry. As noted earlier, these types of contacts are invaluable because they have the knowledge and are motivated through professionalism to understand the issues. Pennsylvania is creeping up the cargo theft analysis charts and many empties from Pennsylvania are found in New Jersey.

The Memphis Auto/Cargo Theft Task Force (TAMCATS) is a multijurisdictional task force composed of local police and sheriff officers and the FBI. This group is busy because the Memphis area has its share of cargo-related incidents. The task force covers the Memphis area along with nearby parts of Arkansas and Mississippi. The group has undergone several makeovers but remains a very good unit. The TAMCATS work closely with the Mid-South Industry Council and maintains a good working public–private partnership.

You can see from this information that cargo task forces are few and far between. It is incumbent upon industry through the national and regional organizations to engage law enforcement in this issue. Providing training, BOLO alerts, and other communication to groups that need them is crucial and many auto theft task forces and auto theft investigators are very receptive to this type of activity.

During the writing of this book, the SWTSC, Hewlett Packard, NICB, and the Texas Department of Public Safety hosted the Texas Cargo Summit. The meeting filled to capacity with 237 attendees; within 2 weeks from the date the summit was announced, it had a waiting list. This shows that cargo theft is relevant and industry and law enforcement people are interested. One of the groups we urged to participate in the summit was the Texas Automobile Burglary Theft Prevention Authority (ABTPA). This organization supports statewide law enforcement task force efforts through auto theft reduction initiatives, education, and public awareness. I have been working with Michelle Lanham, the manager of the Dallas Program, to Reduce Auto Theft (RATT) to involve RATT's task forces

in cargo theft information and training. The ABTPA participated in the Texas Cargo Summit and provided information
about statewide task forces that are available to assist in cargo
theft and commercial vehicle theft recovery. The ABTPA and
Michelle have been very supportive of the SWTSC, its law
enforcement education efforts, and communication network.
By including those tasks forces in information sharing, the
efforts of all entities involved are strengthened. These are the
types of partnerships we like to participate in. Both sides benefit from the interactions.

The SWTSC also established a communication link with the
Texas Motor Transportation Association (TMTA; http://www.
tmta.com/). TMTA receives SWTSC BOLO alerts and SWTSC
receives TMTA information with a mutual understanding that
the theft information sent by TMTA will be sent to the law
enforcement distribution lists of the SWTSC. This is a benefit
for both groups through simple information sharing program
and partnership.

Another relationship the SWTSC finds beneficial in the share
of information is with the **Institute of Scrap Recycling
Industries** (http://www.isri.org). This organization provides
BOLO alerts on metal thefts and groups can sign up to receive
regional notifications. The SWTSC receives information about
scrap recycling incidents. When they are transportation
industry-related, for example, involving a trailer load, we also
send that information to our distribution lists. Partnerships of
public and private organizations that have similar goals are
very attractive and are effective ways to share information and
bring awareness to all interested parties.

There is still much to do and further outreach is needed.
Some organizations need macro views such as the twice
weekly bulletins of SC-ISAC. Others need a more micro view
provided by timely BOLO alerts from the industry council's
communication system. Many other organizations that share
the common goal of preventing cargo theft could benefit from
information-sharing partnerships. As we identify and find those

organizations or they find us, we will continue to build the communication network one person or organization at a time. This is a time-proven successful technique that improves with age and reach. Expanding that reach will always be the main goal for both the industry and law enforcement groups.

Law Enforcement Education

Introduction

Throughout this book we have talked about law enforcement training, specifically teaching law enforcement about our industry, its moving parts, the documentation involved with shipping, and the current crime trends and patterns we determine through our industry-related intelligence-gathering organizations. The law enforcement officers we work with are well trained by their agencies in investigation or and commercial enforcement officers are trained in the areas of regulation and inspection. The training we offer is a supplement to that knowledge and is specific to our industry and how it works.

As many of us are former police officers, we understand investigation from the public side and we also understand the industry. We know how certain information generated by the industry may be beneficial in law enforcement investigations. We also want to teach law enforcement about the methods of cargo crime criminals so that they can be alert to a situation that seems out of place and take action based on knowledge obtained from our training, information, and BOLO alerts.

SWTSC Law Enforcement Training

One training class the SWTSC offers is Cargo Investigation Overview and it covers documentation and operations of interest to law enforcement officers who perform cargo-related investigations or enforcement. It explains the different modes of cargo transportation as discussed in Chapter 2. Understanding operating modes is invaluable, especially when questioning drivers. The training then discusses internal cargo security oversight for industry security management and government compliance issues and programs that apply to the transportation industry. It also covers freight handling and documentation. Understanding the documentation of freight movement is very important to law enforcement investigators because the paper trail provides much information.

The freight industry generates excellent documentation. Every shipment—whether parcel, pallet, or truckload—is traced from origin to destination through company documentation and paperwork required by various departments of transportation. Any shipment can be traced by records showing who picked it up, where it was picked up and from whom, who drove it, who moved it, and who delivered it to whom. All records indicate the times involved with each process:

■ Pick-up and dock-drop documents indicate who picked up material and identified the shipper and location.
■ Manifest documents show handling details (trailer numbers and dock handlers).
■ Line haul and trip sheet information details tractor and trailer data and line drivers.
■ Delivery receipts serve as proof of delivery and identify delivery driver, consignee, and location.

The industry generates thorough paperwork, not to help the police when they serve a subpoena, but because the paper trail provides proof of delivery and thus generates revenue. Training explains the Pro (shipping) number and how that number is the key to obtaining all the other paperwork and identifying the parties involved in a shipment. It is important

for the police investigating a cargo theft to know the participants in shipments, to be able to identify stolen property, and
to understand how transport systems work. The training covers examples of industry records and explains their purposes.

When I conduct training, I advise law enforcement officers
to contact a security or operations person from a company to
help them collect the documentation needed and decipher the
information until they feel comfortable with the process. The
presentation also shows them various types of equipment to
familiarize them with the units, the way they are used, and the
modes that use them. The presentation stresses the way the
industry tracks freight movements via tractor and trailer numbers. If these numbers are provided to company dispatchers
or security personnel, they can immediately determine current
assignment, usage, and location.

Since the police use license plates and vehicle identification numbers (VINs) to enter stolen equipment data into the
National Crime Information Computer (NCIC), a disconnect
can occur between company and law enforcement in reporting a problem. When I worked in the trucking industry, the
companies operated by tractor and trailer numbers. The only
way to obtain registration plate information was to contact
fleet management on the west coast during their business
hours and cross-reference the unit numbers. That meant the
company could not always provide registration information to
police quickly. Teaching police investigators and road officers
to access such information is invaluable. The presentation also
covers company loss reporting, high-value shipment handling,
internal preventative processes, and internal investigative techniques used by company security managers including:

- Tracking devices such as GPS and AGPS
- Radiofrequency (RF) beacons in unmanifested freight for
  driver integrity checks
- Surveillance of drivers and dock workers
- Sting operations using bait trailers and bait freight

The presentation also discusses current criminal methods used by both organized and opportunistic criminal groups that target shippers and carriers including:

■ Truckload theft rings
■ High-value warehouse burglaries
■ Fraudulent and fictitious pick-ups
■ Opportunistic local gangs

If the industry does not present this information to the police, who will? It is incumbent upon the industry to provide this information to law enforcement agencies. The police know how to investigate and do their jobs, but specific knowledge of how an industry operates and perpetrators that victimize it can assist in the success of police investigations and apprehensions.

Another SWTSC law enforcement training course covers its goals and objectives. This presentation is for law enforcement groups that have not worked with the council in the past and it speaks to the council's proposed mission which is "To promote a partnership among carrier security management groups and law enforcement which will enhance communication and cooperation with a focus on transportation security issues, cargo theft and contraband interdiction in Texas and the Southwest area of the United States."

The training also covers membership of the council: "Security management groups from companies involved in the transportation field and law enforcement personnel assigned to units which investigate shipment (cargo), vehicle, and commercial vehicle theft or conduct commercial vehicle enforcement or interdiction." The presentation then discusses operating principles, objectives, and goals of the council:

Principles
Status as a non-profit 501(c)6 voluntary organization
Dedication to cargo security and transportation issues
Inclusion of all modes of transportation

Membership composed of shippers, carriers, insurers, warehousing, forwarders, and vendors

Law enforcement networking and education

Objectives

Improve cargo transportation security

Serve as clearinghouse for information for Southwest cargo issues

Platform for Southwest cargo security matters

Assist voluntary initiatives by government and the private sector

Goals

Increase communication between law enforcement and transportation security

Promote exchange of security-related information between companies and law enforcement

Provide assistance and training to law enforcement

Provide education on supply chain methods and documentation

Assistance with major recoveries

Assistance with theft stings

Develop law enforcement networks to provide alerts and information related to cargo security and theft

Assist law enforcement with interdiction of illegal drug shipments in commercial carriers through company training and customer profiling

Interdiction: Company Operation and Documentation is another presentation developed by SWTSC for law enforcement. This training covers commercial trucking interdiction, shows established profiles for contraband shipping, and discusses the different modes of transportation and makes other points about freight transportation detailed below.

No matter which mode is used, all shipment movement originates and is delivered by truck. Although this information is elementary, it is important to understand in dealing with non-truck modes. It adds layers to the movement that smugglers do not like.

Commercial trucking is a safe way for drug traffickers to move large amounts of contraband. Drug traffickers like commercial transportation since it insulates them from the contraband and may allow easier passage through Border Patrol checkpoints, especially in the LTL mode.

Trucking company policies can actually assist drug traffickers. The director of one company I worked for set a rule that if contraband was found, security managers had to notify the shipper. This type of rule eliminates law enforcement options including conducting reverse deliveries and identifying traffickers. If I were a trafficker and could identify a company with this type of asinine rule, I would use it to ship all my contraband and eliminate most of my risk.

Internet shipment tracking acts as a trafficker's accomplice and constitutes another Internet advantage for them. All shipments are now tracked via the Internet so customers can follow their progress. Before the Internet systems, found contraband could be diverted to law enforcement and they could plan a reverse delivery upon arrival at a destination. Now the shipment tracking has to be kept in place even if a shipment is diverted so the traffickers will not be aware that a shipment has been interdicted. Security management needs to work with law enforcement to assist with the Internet tracking charade when needed.

Company systems and shipments are also covered in training, specifically:

Every shipment is tracked from pick-up to final delivery. Every detail of movement is detailed (who handled cargo and when). For investigative follow-up, this information is available through company security managers or can be obtained through a subpoena after a legal action is started. Every document related to a shipment can be produced.

Unknown shippers are not allowed to place shipments into the supply chain. Before September 11, 2001, unknown shippers existed but that is no longer possible.

Most companies assist law enforcement with delivery of contraband with some restrictions if concerns about employee safety and hazards at company facilities are observed. However, some companies will not allow any form of assistance on their property.

An important part of the training discusses the paperwork continuum of a shipment:

The original shipment receipt showing dock drop or yard entry data is a bill of lading (BOL) listing cargo, shipper, and consignee (receiver).

The origin information is detailed in manifests generated at the origin location indicating freight receipt, handlers, and unit numbers.

At intermediate locations, loading and off-loading manifests list handlers and trailer numbers.

At the destination location, loading and off-loading manifests indicate freight handlers and trailer numbers. Pick-up and delivery (P&D) trip sheets show manifest, driver, and time information A delivery receipt or proof of delivery (POD) shows time of delivery, driver, and signature of consignee (receiver).

Examples of the documents are presented and basic tractor and trailer equipment information is reviewed. After that, known drug shipment profiles are discussed:

Origin from Southern locations—Most shipments are placed into commercial freight systems from southern locations on the US side of the Mexican border.

Placement into system through dock drop at origin—Shipments are often brought to the dock by a representative of the shipper. At this point most companies capture the representative's identification by entering the shipment and the vehicle license plate number of the vehicle that brought the shipment to the yard.

Use of company name or known customer information—Shippers often use a current customer name and some even use preprinted BOLs from known customers.

Payments with cash, prepaid credit card, or designation of cash collection at destination—These payment methods are hard to trace or tie to financial records. Many companies have stopped using cash collection.

Carrier's receipt of numerous calls during shipment to check on arrival—Before Internet tracking became routine, traffickers would constantly call a terminal to see whether their shipments arrived. With Internet tracking, they call to see whether their shipments are ready for pick-up as soon as the shipments are shown to arrive at their destinations..

Securely packed shipments—Packaging in wooden crates, placement of straps, lack of transparency, and sealants or caulks in the seams of boxes, barrels, and crates are clues to illicit shipments. The photographs In this chapter illustrate the packaging methods used for illicit shipments. Remember, shipping is charged by weight so most legitimate shippers (unlike traffickers) make their shipments as light as possible.

BOL description does not match packaging—This is an important point. Traffickers sometimes declare to ship items that are cheaper to buy at the destination rather than ship.

Product description does not match weight or shipment size—Washer and dryers that weigh 300 to 400 pounds are unusual items and require attention by dock personnel. A product description that is not consistent with weight, shipment size, or item description along with a lack of transparency is a big giveaway.

Auto parts shipments—Traffickers frequently use auto parts as covers for product descriptions and shipping and consignee company names. One reason is that auto parts cover the weight issue better than many other products. Any "auto part" shipment packed In a 3/4-Inch plywood wooden crate with 3-inch screws is probably not legitimate, particularly if It shows caulking in the seams or has the odor of dryer sheets.

Freight designated for dock pick-up or false delivery address—Shipments designated for pick-up at a shipping dock may contain illegal goods. A fraudulent consignee address may be an empty lot or vacant house. Delivery to a false address is dangerous to a driver. Drivers are not supposed to make outside deliveries under these conditions, but in such circumstances it may be safer for a driver to deliver than to try to refuse.

Use of prepaid cell phone and phone cards—Traffickers frequently use these communications to prevent detection because prepaid phones and credit cards do not tie an individual to their use.

After listing some significant points and profiles of contraband shipments, the SWTSC training presents drug shipment photos gathered from members. The photos show shipments containing illicit narcotics that were interdicted during transport. The LTL companies that provided them were willing to share their information with the council and allow the photos to be used in training. The photos are now the intellectual property of the SWTSC. When contraband shipments are found, most of the points made above are factors in the crime. The shipment shown in Figure 5.1 was identified by the weight discrepancy along with several other profiles listed above. This packaging provides the trafficker one of the most important necessities: no transparency.

The box shown in Figure 5.2 was listed as containing tools and once again this shipment included several of the profile points above including a dock drop, a cash payment, and the weight of the shipping container. If several of the points above relate to a shipment, it most likely will contain contraband.

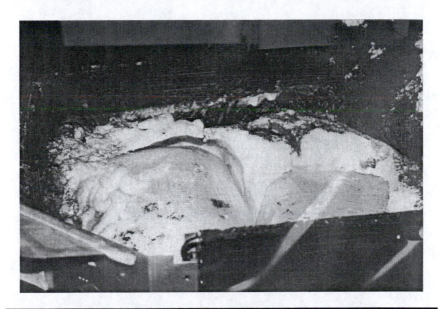

Figure 5.1 Marijuana hidden in air conditioner as cover for transport in a commercial transportation vehicle. (*Source:* Coughlin, J.J. SWTSC's Interdiction: Company Operation and Documentation presentation. With permission.)

Figure 5.2 Package placed in commercial shipping lane and labeled as tools shows the lack of transparency found in contraband shipments. (*Source:* Coughlin, J.J. SWTSC's Interdiction: Company Operation and Documentation presentation. With permission.)

The occurrence depicted in Figures 5.3 and 5.4 is rare and several of the above factors assisted in this discovery. The smugglers bundled narcotics in liquid-proof packaging and dropped them into the Gaylord shipment pallet. They poured some type of liquid clay over the narcotics and allowed it to harden. The method was ingenious but the smugglers'

Figure 5.3 Narcotics bundled in waterproof packaging covered with liquid clay after placement in Gaylord shipping pallet.

Figure 5.4   Narcotics bundled in waterproof packaging covered with liquid clay after placement in Gaylord shipping pallet.

problems arose from their description of contents, the dock drop, and cash collection of payment. When you put these profiles together, contraband is involved 95% of the time.

Figure 5.5 shows a strapped and sealed pallet covered with black shrink-wrap. This is a real attempt to eliminate transparency. On the right is the BOL (carrier company information removed) listing satellite parts. The shipment raised several flags. First, the weight was 965 pounds—a little heavy for satellite parts—and the BOL cited a dock-drop shipment. Real shippers never package their freight so well. Remember, shipping costs are determined by weight and preparing a shipment for shipping is also a production cost. A lot of density is required for a box this size to weigh 965 pounds. An overwrapped and overpackaged box is a definite flag for contraband.

The barrel shipment shown in Figure 5.6 involved mismatched description and weight and a few of the other factors cited above. A significant flag was the use of a caulk or sealant on the lid. Such sealing of lids and seams of barrels, crates, and other containers almost always indicates that a shipper is trying to conceal the true identity of the declared contents. Figure 5.7 and Figure 5.8 show a contraband shipment trifecta

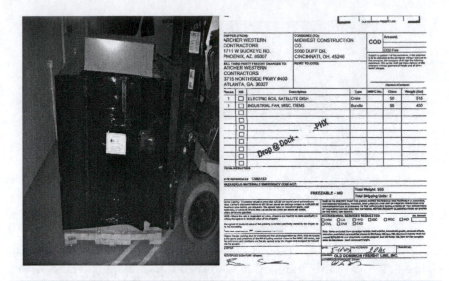

Figure 5.5 Satellite parts that weigh far too much, are not transparent, and fit several other profiles including dock drop as documented on the BOL. (*Source:* Coughlin, J.J. SWTSC's Interdiction: Company Operation and Documentation presentation. With permission.)

Figure 5.6 Bundled drugs sealed in a barrel for shipment. Relevant points were no transparency and a weight problem based on information on BOL. (*Source:* Coughlin, J.J. SWTSC's Interdiction: Company Operation and Documentation presentation. With permission.)

Figure 5.7 Auto parts shipper and consignee were named. Package has black shrink-wrap and no transparency.

on the packaging side. Figure 5.7 shows the outside of the wrapped package—a 3/4-inch homemade plywood crate covered in black shrink-wrap addressed to an auto repair shop. The description on the BOL was "car parts." Figure 5.8 shows how the narcotics were individually wrapped and placed in a container with caulking or sealant around the seams. This shipment almost hit every profile point listed. This type of packaging for a common product almost always contains contraband.

Figure 5.9 and Figure 5.10 show another contraband shipment interdicted by awareness of the profiles listed above. These wire reels were stuffed with marijuana bricks that skewed the weight. The shipment also raised several other flags that made employees and security management more than a little curious. The washer shown in Figure 5.11 was loaded with bricks of marijuana. The weight of the shipment was a huge flag.

Figure 5.8 Overpackaging in heavy homemade wooden crate. (*Source:* **Coughlin, J.J. SWTSC's Interdiction: Company Operation and Documentation presentation. With permission.)**

Weight of product and description are frequent contraband flags. A BOL description of a product that would be cheaper to buy at the destination is a clue. The cost of transporting the heavily loaded washer in Figure 5.11 made the cost at destination way out of line. One incident involved a shipper that listed contraband as lawn chairs. The weight was a mismatch. The shipping cost made new lawn chairs far cheaper. See Figure 5.12.

Packaging that is too good should be considered an exception. Dock workers tell me that they spend much more time repackaging poorly packed legitimate cargo; they spend little time repackaging perfectly crated and sealed shipments.

The shippers of the crate in Figure 5.13 wrote the address with a black felt marker. The crate was designated for an auto

Figure 5.9 Drugs stuffed inside wire spindles. Weight issues and lack of transparency are clues. (*Source:* Coughlin, J.J. SWTSC's Interdiction: Company Operation and Documentation presentation. With permission.)

body shop destination. Figure 5.14 shows the bundles of marijuana found inside the crate. All of the shipments we have looked at came from southern terminals near the border—another point of the profile.

Several photos show details of a package delivered to an LTL company for shipment from California to Georgia. The BOL described the freight as ice cream machines. Figure 5.14 depicts how the machines were delivered to the LTL Company. Figure 5.15 and Figure 5.16 show the canisters and motor parts. The methamphetamine bags (50 pounds) pulled from the canisters inside the ice cream machines are shown in Figure 5.17. This shipment fit several of the profile points including a dock-drop shipment, a prepaid credit card, and discrepancies in the consignee name and address.

Figure 5.10 Drugs stuffed inside wire spindles. Weight issues and lack of transparency are clues. (*Source:* Coughlin, J.J. SWTSC's Interdiction: Company Operation and Documentation presentation. With permission.)

Handling Contraband

Now that you have a good indication of the profiles of contraband shipments, you must consider how you would handle one when discovered. After teaching frontline dock employees the indicators of contraband shipments, you will quickly start identifying suspicious packages. Freight companies have a right to inspect any package accepted into their shipping systems. Laws against search and seizure are very strict. This is very important to understand so that contraband can be confiscated and taken into police custody without evidentiary problems.

Treatment of a suspicious shipment or package must be done correctly in case the law enforcement agencies decide to pursue reverse delivery options and prosecution. Certain rules

Figure 5.11 Drugs stuffed into top-load washer. No transparency. Washer heavier than normal weight. (*Source:* Coughlin, J.J. SWTSC's Interdiction: Company Operation and Documentation presentation. With permission.)

should be followed when a package appears suspicious. The best progression would be first identifying a package through paperwork, suspicion, viewing a shipment, and combining all three factors. An employee who notes a suspicious package should notify the local terminal manager so that all details can be reviewed. If the suspicions remain, the employee should immediately involve the security manager or person designated to review such circumstances.

Here is the "catch 22" relative to the legality of search and seizure. If company personnel have suspicions and search the package and find contraband, this is legal and when reported to the authorities they now do not need a search warrant for the package. If, while relying on your suspicions based on the

Figure 5.12 Homemade wooden crate described to hold car parts; consignee was automotive operation. (*Source:* Coughlin, J.J. SWTSC's Interdiction: Company Operation and Documentation presentation. With permission.)

Figure 5.13 Homemade wooden crate described to hold car parts; consignee was automotive operation. (*Source:* Coughlin, J.J. SWTSC's Interdiction: Company Operation and Documentation presentation. With permission.)

Figure 5.14   How ice cream machines were tendered to LTL transporter.

Figure 5.15   Black cylinder canister above is the search target.

aforementioned profile and related facts, you do not search the package but instead notify law enforcement, the ball is now in their court. If they direct you to search the package, this makes you their agent in the eyes of the law and the subsequent finding of the contraband would be an illegal search and seizure. Based on this information, you need to either search based on your training and suspicions or report it to the law enforcement agents and have them come to the dock

Figure 5.16 Fifty pounds of methamphetamine were found inside these two motor parts of an ice cream machine.

Figure 5.17 Bags of methamphetamine stuffed in ice cream machine parts.

Figure 5.18 Drug-sniffing law enforcement dock helper and cargo buster.

to conduct their own investigation to determine if they have probable cause to obtain a warrant to search the package. Of course, as part of their establishment of probable cause, they could use the known drug shipment profiles listed above as part of the justification.

Many law enforcement responders use drug dogs like the one pictured in Figure 5.18 to find the probable cause needed to open a package. After a suspicious package is brought to the attention of management, it should be moved to a section of the dock where it can be overseen but does not interfere with operations. When the police arrive, they will take possession of the shipment until a determination can be made. If a shipment is contraband, the police will take possession of the shipment, ask for related documents, and discuss with the company the strategy and options available.

Often after identifying a contraband shipment, analyzing shipper, consignee, and locations for pick-up and delivery, you may be able to identify past shipments that may be related and identify receivers. If this information is shared with other carriers, it can yield information on other shipments and drug conspiracies. If law enforcement officials follow this path, the security manager or designate should assist the officers to obtain information through the company legal office, usually by subpoena.

Drug traffickers use many different transportation companies but their methods are pretty consistent. Much information is provided in freight documents and documents from multiple shipments will be helpful to law enforcement. The SWTSC partnered with the Drug Enforcement Agency and several of its agents to ensure that member companies experiencing trafficking problems have immediate contacts for referral. I have taught interdiction classes to several groups of DEA personnel in Houston and Dallas to help them understand the company side of the equation. Especially in the southern border region, company security managers should establish a relationship with drug enforcement agents in the jurisdictions where their terminals are located so that when the issues arise, they will already have contacts and plans for handling suspicious packages.

Council members have had better responses using federal level agents instead of locals in the southern border region. If smugglers put contraband into your system and it moves, federal agents have much broader jurisdiction and better capabilities. The DEA office in Houston assigned Mark Walicki to work with the council as part of its federal initiative. This relationship worked very well and led to successful major investigations and conspiracy cases prosecuted by the DEA.

These situations can come to the attention of the companies or law enforcement in many ways. It is incumbent upon both sides to work together to prevent the use of the commercial shipping lanes from abuse by traffickers. Furthermore, the inclusion of illicit materials in commercial systems puts legitimate company employees unknowingly in harm's way during pick-up, transit, or delivery.

The placing of contraband in commercial vehicle systems has gone on since the invention of the wheel. Moving unacceptable or illegal materials is commonplace. Smugglers will use extreme methods to get their goods to their markets. Smuggling balloons

In my 10 years working for a transportation company, I assisted law enforcement with several cases involving drug smuggling. Most cases started when an employee identified a suspicious package in transit and assisted law enforcement with interdiction and reverse deliveries before company policy changes made cooperating with law enforcement difficult. One unique case involved a customer of our freight airline in a border city in Texas. The customer had an account with our airline and used preprinted airway bills for normal shipments.

During an audit, the customer discovered 12 shipments over a period of 8 months that were billed to its account but did not match its shipping records. The terminal manager met with company staff and reviewed the information. He notified our security department and I was assigned the investigation since it was in my region. I compiled all the paperwork on the phantom shipments. The suspect had to be an employee because he or she used the customer's preprinted airway bills to place the shipment into the system. Every shipment was entered into the system via a scanner that was used on the dock and not assigned to a particular employee. All the shipments were in the 500-pound weight range, traveled to locations in the midwest and noted as dock pick-ups. There were no records of a shipper or vehicle coming to the dock around the scanning times of the phantom shipments. This was one of the first hints of a contraband shipment.

I reviewed employee records for the dates of the shipments and compared shipment dates to determine which employees were present on all the days in question. This lowered our pool of suspect employees to a manageable number. During my deep background checks of potential employee suspects, a federal investigator contacted me about some of the shipments. We were able compare information about the internal suspects and share information about the other shipments. Due to law enforcement involvement, the employee was eventually identified and indicted along with several other traffickers. The company lost revenue on the 12 shipments and the investigation later revealed that the suspect employee was paid by the traffickers to handle the shipments. This was my only case involving both traffickers and an internal partner. Their connection allowed the illicit shipments to be easily entered into the system without normal scrutiny.

Many cases involved our LTL companies. In one incident, I was notified by law enforcement officers that they observed one of our trucks pick up a shipment (pallet) at a location under surveillance for drug trafficking in South Texas. They were able to provide license plate numbers on the truck and trailer and a time and location of pick-up. Note that law enforcement information utilized license plate information instead of unit trailer or tractor numbers as discussed earlier. Based on this information, I identified the shipment in question, the shipper, and other pertinent information. The shipment picked up by my company and observed by law enforcement was already en route to our Dallas break bulk facility. I notified law enforcement of the scheduled arrival time of the shipment and officers went to the Dallas dock to inspect the package. As they waited for the shipment to arrive, I continued my search and found several other shipments that the shipper placed in our system previously that were probably going to be of interest to the police. When the shipment arrived, law enforcement inspected it and obtained a search warrant to open the package. They found hundreds of pounds of marijuana. They took control of the shipment and continued their investigation. The shipment data from our company assisted the law enforcement investigation. When I sought shipment information relating to use of a pick-up location by other LTL companies based on an SWTSC inquiry, law enforcement was able to identify many previous illicit shipments and the information helped them pursue a conspiracy and organized drug investigation involving many parties.

of heroin in the anal cavity or swallowing them to get through inspections is not new. This activity will go on long after this writing and those who test the systems will continue to try to find better, less detectable ways to move contraband.

The profiles we discussed earlier have been consistent in the transportation industry for years and they seldom change. We have seen a move to harder-to-trace prepaid phones, prepaid credit card payments, and other technology that assists traffickers in protecting their true identities. The ability to use the Internet to trace shipments is a boon to those who want to follow their illicit booty from point to point. We know that as drugs move north and pass the Border Patrol checkpoints, they gain value. The profiles listed earlier in this chapter represent information every supply chain operator and every law officer who deals in contraband activities should know.

Parties that try to move contraband in commercial vehicles continue to meet the profiles discussed above. If terrorists want to use commercial vehicles to transport weapons of mass destruction or their components, the same profiles will come into play. They prepare their packages without transparency, falsify the contents descriptions, overwrap packages, track packages frequently until they arrive, and use prepaid phone and credit cards. The techniques work for any and all contraband. The biggest problem arises because the packages originate in many places. For that reason, the profile information needs to reach everyone who needs to know. In a commercial entity, every person from top to bottom, from CEO to cleaning crew, should be aware of suspicious items or activities. Security and awareness must be included in a company's overall culture to achieve the best and most efficient results.

Conclusion

The training developed by members of the SWTSC has been taught to many law enforcement officers over the years. The classes are not designed to teach the police how to investigate. They are designed to inform police about the industry and the work of the industry councils. After working in law enforcement and in the cargo industry, I realize the important role industry paperwork plays in law enforcement investigations, especially in smuggling cases. It is vital to provide industry overviews to law enforcement officers so that are aware of the sources and resources available to them. The SWTSC even sends law enforcement officers to other cargo training schools and conferences via scholarships and funding. This builds the public–private partnership in a very solid way. Now that we have talked about law enforcement training, we can focus on best practices in the industry.

Chapter 6

Prevention and Awareness

Introduction

After looking at the many risks, threats, and obstacles which can be found in the supply chain, we need to look at the many ways we can use prevention, technology, and awareness to build an efficient and effective system for each business unit to have the best chance to succeed against the known and the unexpected. The U. S. Government released the first information on a national strategy for global supply chain security on January 23, 2012. In this strategy, the government wrote about undertaking a number of efforts to strengthen the global supply chain including legislative requirements (regulation) and a number of strategic efforts with a specific security focus, where they footnoted fourteen different laws and acts which have been passed since 2002. Although I believe it is beneficial to have a strategic government program, this macro vision of the plans leaves most of us who work in the industry wanting more information concerning the operational grassroots working on the implementation. In looking at the government's "path forward" bullet points, as part of their aligning federal activities, I would suggest they consider sponsoring or participating in cargo theft task forces, assisting the set-up and financing of such task forces in those parts of the country where the volume of cargo crime justifies the investment. I believe that if the government worked at the grassroots level from the domestic side out, they would understand risk and threats better than ever, which goes to the second point of refining their understanding of threats and risks associated with the supply chain. I believe that they should also closely look at the national strategy proposed by the National Cargo Theft Task Force (NCTTF) and incorporate some of those proposals into their plan. The NCTTF plan seeks many things which would work in concert with the government's plan and provide a more direct support to the industry from an operational level.

The NCTTF strategy calls for the government to define its role and responsibilities for federal agencies' involvement in cargo theft investigation, intelligence gathering, interagency cooperation, resources for state and local agency participation, and intergovernmental agency data sharing. The plan would connect existing cargo theft task forces and develop others in key regions where they are needed. Most importantly, in my estimation, the plan calls for enhanced information sharing and intelligence collection. This information share needs to include industry and public information and not be restricted to a law enforcement or government secret network. There can be tiers to protect law enforcement's sensitive information, but the systems need to share information effectively to get it to persons who need to know.

The NCTTF also proposes that the need for funding be directed to the task forces to pay for equipment and overtime while asking for the laws to be enhanced for cargo crime punishment. Both plans call for threat assessments and the NCTTF would like cargo theft to be a part of the assessment beyond the government plan, which was more related to intentional attacks, accidents, and natural disasters.

If these two strategies were combined and unnecessary regulation and redundancy were eliminated along with a robust industry partnership, the program would be a huge benefit for all parties. Federal law enforcement has had a very small role in cargo theft investigation for quite some time, and it would be good to see them engage on a much higher level in a crime that so often involves interstate activity and organized criminal enterprises.

Prevention: The Best policy

The reality is that prevention and awareness start with each and every individual company or participant in the supply chain. I tell industry people all of the time that it is best not to count on any government agency for anything. The police are not your recovery plan, and the government's National Strategy of Global Supply Chain Security is not your prevention or operation plan. Each company should set its own standards of prevention, awareness, security, and safety. No one knows your company needs or operation better than you do. I would much rather set a policy based on my operational needs than on some government mandate. Many government mandates come to fruition though because companies choose to overlook a true need. To have a security prevention program, guidelines must be set for every part of the business where security considerations should be a part of the operation. This would include:

- ■ Human Resources
  - – Training and Orientation
- ■ Business Partner Requirements/Vendor Management
- ■ Facility Security
- ■ Procedural Security
- ■ In-Transit Security
- ■ Brokerage (if applicable)
- ■ IT Security
- ■ Legal Best Practices

All of these may not apply to each and everyone's business or operation, but each one that is part of your operation should be addressed. We will look at each of these areas when we discuss the best practices a bit later in the chapter. There are discussions to be had on each and case examples, which will show the reasoning for these guidelines or regulations to be put in writing and made a formal part of the company process. Many companies have the best of intentions, but fail to lay out specific written plans for each part of their operations. I see this lacking in many areas of security. Ask a company for its written security plan and recovery plan and watch for the very empty look. I would not hire or deal with a company that does not have a designated security manager or, preferably, a team or that does not have a written security plan and security training and awareness as part of employee orientation. If you find a company with these in place, you will probably not have many issues or conflicts and if you do, you will be able to deal with someone who actually can resolve your problem. I have had many people tell me that security is a cash burn and not a revenue generator. Not true. If done correctly, what you spend on security will pay off in multiples. Not all security solutions cost money; many are just processes, procedures, and efforts. It is the small things which many times count. Crossing the T's and dotting the I's go a long way in the security world. Understanding the risks and threats and setting policy to protect the operation gives you the best chance to succeed.

First Annual Texas Cargo Summit

During the final two days, I had the privilege of attending the First Annual Texas Cargo Summit. This summit was put together by the Southwest Transportation Security Council, Hewlett Packard, the National Insurance Crime Bureau, and the Texas Department of Public Safety. Being part of the coordination of this summit and assisting with getting this program together was a lot of work, yet much fun. This was our first effort in Texas to provide industry and law enforcement a two-day venue for training specific to the cargo theft issue. The presenters included both law enforcement officers and industry practitioners. The majority of the presentations spoke to the points of prevention.

The first training session concerned the Southern border. Most industry operators do not understand the problems and issues of operating near the border. It has its own dynamic and creates a curiosity for those who are in the industry, but who do not live or work in that environment. When we look at cargo stats, we see that the border areas are not major problems. There is no issue of major cargo theft occurring in the United States and the cargo going to Mexico. The issue for the industry has always been the loss of equipment, tractors and trailers, and those pieces going south never to be seen again. The theft of supply chain and heavy equipment that is then taken into Mexico is a problem. The Texas Department of Public Safety and border departments work with Mexico's law enforcement to try to repatriate stolen units back to the United States. The drug cartels are much more involved in moving drugs and people illegally north than being involved in theft in the United States going back into Mexico. There is plenty of cargo theft in Mexico but, so far, cross-border theft has not been a major issue. This presentation put some myths to rest and reinforced the fact that cross-border cargo theft is currently not a major issue, unlike the equipment theft.

Being from Texas and working here throughout my different careers, I am asked about the border quite often. Moving freight across the border has its ingrained processes involving custom brokers and U.S. entry. Many people just want to understand those things. There are border ports of entry, and there are internal border patrol check points. Each has different responsibilities and is operated by different federal law enforcement agencies and mean different things to freight companies. We will look to address different issues and have different presenters discuss these issues in the future.

The second presentation came from CargoNet, a Verisk Analytics Company which in 2009, through ISO and the National Insurance Crime Bureau (NICB), collaborated to create a national information-sharing system to combat cargo theft. They designed a system that enables more efficient, accurate, and timely sharing of cargo theft information among theft victims, their insurers, and law enforcement.

CargoNet established a nationally coordinated data-sharing system which takes into account the needs of insurers, law enforcement, transportation companies, manufacturers, retailers, and their many agents and service providers. The core of the network is a new database called CargoNet. The program focuses on aggregating and sharing information and intelligence from multiple task forces, other police agencies, and the industry. CargoNet uses case management and analytic functions that will enhance the effectiveness of cargo theft task forces and law enforcement. The network will also encompass training and investigative support for law enforcement, as well as theft prevention services and analytics. The presenters were Keith Lewis of CargoNet and Fred Lohmann of the National Insurance Crime Bureau. They spoke of the aforementioned collaboration and gave insight into the system and how its database and information could be very informative and helpful in cargo theft and cargo fraud cases. Any law enforcement agent or officer can gain access for free, and tapping into this intelligence source will be very helpful when conducting investigations.

The third presenter was Detective Ivy Haley from the Fort Worth Police Department, who is assigned to commercial vehicle theft in the Auto Theft Unit. Ivy has been a very good partner to the council and the industry and she works diligently on cargo and industry investigations. During her presentation, she discussed several successful arrests and investigations. She also spoke to the many frustrations that come when companies don't have the best practices. She made several points to industry where they could improve themselves. Once police investigators have been around the industry and have become involved with the councils and attend the training events, they get a pretty good handle on the basics. They truly understand how to investigate the cargo side and realize what paperwork and information to look for. They know to look for cameras at the victim company or nearby to try to catch a glimpse of the act and they know, based on the same factors we talked about earlier, which set of suspects they may be looking for. Beyond that, not having actually worked internally within the industry, they really do not exactly know what companies do or don't do when it comes to security. All companies are not the same and based on their specific operation, do things very differently. Most large well-established companies have pretty robust security operations and management teams. These security professionals work diligently to protect their company's assets. They are

I was attending a Miami–Dade Police TOMCATS Cargo Theft School in Miami in 2007 and one of the presenters was a former member of their task force. During his presentation, he blurted out that companies "do not know sh—!" This was not very professional and, in reality, was coming from someone who had never worked for a company, someone totally without knowledge. It is easy to point fingers and give advice when you do not have to factor in practicality and cost. Since I worked on both sides of the fence, I have a better understanding of what the police can do and what the companies can do and both make pretty good efforts the majority of the times. We really need to work at having a good public/private partnership, which is what industry councils and information sharing are all about.

able to adjust to the changing threats in the industry. Some smaller companies are not able to accomplish as much.

The next presenter, John Tabor of National Retail Systems, gave a presentation about their security program and operation. Where Ivy had pointed out some deficiencies of companies in her talk, John showed how a company can be in control of its entire operation using a yard management system integrated into the overall security plan. John is a very entertaining speaker and his presentation represented how National Retail Systems as a company deals with issues. John is very involved in the industry councils and cargo theft law enforcement circles. He is on the board of the National Cargo Theft Task Force and is a supporter of these types of events. His presentation explained how companies accomplish an efficient security program when they put in the effort and it was a counterpunch to Ivy's presentation, not in a negative way, but showing the different ways in how things can be done. After watching the two presentations, the point you would probably get is that the companies that make the better effort need the police much less often than those that don't. John's presentation makes the point of this chapter which is about the need for prevention and how security prevention saves time and money in the long run. National Retail Systems has had security issues in the past; after having those challenges, it made the adjustments to its security operation to prevent further problems. John's presentation stressed prevention, smart security, and follow through.

The second day of the conference started with a program from the Texas Department of Public Safety. The presentation, conducted by Lt. Randy Stewart, dealt with a specific group of Cubans who had drifted to Texas and started a small splinter cargo theft crew in Hunt County. This is indicative of what we were identifying from the cargo theft stats in Texas. Four or five years ago, we were seeing the organized in-transit thefts and finding all of the empty and abandoned equipment in Florida or Georgia. This group in Texas was working from this area and not going back to Florida with each theft. There are splinter groups like these in New Jersey, Kentucky, Texas, and other places which are being identified bit by bit from the data analysis. In this case, the Texas Department of Public Safety District One investigators were able to obtain over a dozen indictments for group members and eventually shut down their Texas splinter operation. The presentation tied together the local pieces and showed the independence of the crew from the Florida influence. It is too early to tell, but these cargo criminals may not like the sentences they receive from some of these rural county juries. If they are going to splinter out, they may want to hang in the large, metropolitan counties where property crime justice is routinely overlooked. This is a fairly new phenomenon which investigators around the country may want to start checking. Remember: the location of the empties is going to be one of the first best indicators of a splinter group operation.

The next presentation was conducted by two local National Insurance Crime Bureau agents, Jerry Allen and Stacy Hohenberger. They laid out the grassroots view of the NICB cargo theft program. Both agents are sworn officers embedded in law enforcement units with cargo theft and insurance fraud as their main responsibilities. They are a major part of the information sharing and law enforcement intelligence locally. They provide assistance to law enforcement and work for NICB member companies. Their presentation laid out an overview of the cargo theft problem and the assistance they are able to give. They also discussed the CargoNet product and capabilities since NICB is a part of the collaboration with ISO for CargoNet. No company or entity has made a bigger push into the cargo theft arena than NICB has in the past several years. They are in position and very willing to help in cargo theft investigations and the coordination of law enforcement and industry efforts.

Following NICB was Shawn Driscoll, director of security for Swift Transportation. He presented an overview of the

Swift Security Department, explaining how it operates and the impact it has had on the company issues. During his presentation, he explained how Swift experienced thirty-five (35) full trailer load thefts in 1997. The company started a security focus in response to those incidents and, within a few years, had reduced the losses to a small number. Swift purchased another carrier that had not been using best practices in hiring and other areas, and the first year after the merger Swift found itself with twenty-two major thefts. Using the same security focus and best practices on the new carrier, within a few years, Swift had the full trailer load losses back down to one for year 2011. His presentation demonstrated a security department which applied best practices from the hiring process on. Swift has a system of tracking its equipment and loads and takes great pride in controlling both drivers and the fleet. His presentation was a testament to prevention and best practices, again showing how you can make a direct effect on your company's bottom line through process and procedure.

After lunch, Scott Cornell, head of Travelers Insurance Special Investigative Group (SIG) which works Cargo Theft investigations for its customers, came to the podium. Travelers has been in the cargo theft arena for many years and has participated at all levels and across the country in the information sharing and education. Travelers has a large team of investigators across the country that can conduct insurance investigations and assist industry and law enforcement. Travelers has many additional capabilities including a forensic evidence lab and other analytical tools which it offers for investigative assistance. The company also works closely with the National Insurance Crime Bureau in supporting covert investigative tools for cargo theft task forces and investigators.

In many cargo cases, there are many people with skin in the game. You have the shipper, the carriers, insurers, and the consignee. Each of these parties may have different insurance representatives. One cargo case could bring many different groups into the investigation on the private side, not counting the public responders. Much of what these conferences accomplish is to unite those resources to work together, to know each other and to understand the capabilities of each distinct group. This knowledge and understanding allow many cases to enter into several intelligence systems and work across industry and law enforcement to provide the best chance for recovery if your processes do fail. Even a few short years ago, this collaboration was not nearly as strong as it is now. It still has room to grow, but it has been fun watching it come together over time and having successes more and more often.

Next I did a presentation looking at the 2010 and 2011 Supply Chain-Information Sharing and Analysis Center Cargo Theft charts. We looked at those charts and walked the audience through the analysis, even being able to refer to previous charts and information. I do this type of presentation for many different audiences throughout the year and, depending on the group, I stress different things. The fact that this group was composed of about sixty percent law enforcement, most of whom had not been involved in this issue, allowed me to walk them through the charts and analysis and explain to the audience what they mean. The charts reveal the most prolific cargo theft states, the types of locations that host the most thefts, the days of the week cargo criminals prefer to strike, and the items or commodities they target. Like the old board game, Clue, it gives you "Mr. Mustard in the kitchen with a knife" scenario. When you look at the South Florida organized gangs, the key to the cargo theft analysis starts with the commodity. The target is always the product in the truck, followed by where it is first left unattended, and it really doesn't matter whether that is a truck stop, carrier facility, secured yard, or street. The involved state will be within the first need to stop for the driver of the load. So in "Clue" game jargon you could say, "Mr. S. Floridian in the truck stop with a load of electronics using his ignition puller" or "Mr. Armenian with a load of meat using identity theft." This may sound elementary, but in many cases, it is very true. We also discussed different methods of operation out there currently and how that methodology has changed during the last five years.

A key to understanding the identity of the possible suspects is the location where the empty equipment trailer is recovered. This has allowed us to see changing of tractors right after the crime, painting over trailers, and identifying splinter groups operating in locations other than Florida. The charts are not just numbers; they usually tell us a story and allow us to see those small deviations that give us a better chance to recover and prevent.

The next presenters were from Hewlett Packard, the conference location host. Their presentation, led by Bob Gammon and Kevin Mazza, provided great information about what HP could do for law enforcement investigators. This is not only important information from one shipper, it also relays information about what could be expected from like organizations. When property is recovered, law enforcement needs to know what information its agents need to provide to a manufacturer or shipper if they expect to track that property to the correct owner or complainant. It was a short presentation but contained very valuable information.

So, after looking at this two-day program, you see many variables, but also good information and networking. Many industries and law enforcement agencies will join the industry council or SC-ISAC, and start getting the BOLO/Alerts and/or weekly bulletins which will bring awareness to the issue. Nothing but good can come from this type of conference, and we plan on putting one together for next year. This entire event was about awareness and prevention and building our law enforcement networks.

Several years ago I put together a best practices document for the Southwest Transportation Security Council. It took into account most of the information we have discussed so far in this book and also looked at legal points based on the additions provided by Mr. Steve Lewis of Dallas, our Council's legal advisor and transportation attorney. The best practices document was a bullet point list with the aforementioned categories we looked at earlier. Let's take those points and expound on each as we relate them to the information we have discussed thus far.

The first section of the SWTSC Best Supply Chain Security Practices starts with personnel security.

Personnel Security

Companies of all transportation modes should:

■ Conduct pre-employment background investigation to include criminal history, social security validation, employment history, and drug screens. (Make sure you use quality background checks that are FCRA compliant and not just database checks.)

■ Periodically check current employees for criminal history, driver's license status and random or suspicious behavior drug screens.

■ Maintain a current permanent employee list, which includes the name, date of birth, social security number, and position held.

■ Have procedures in place to remove company identification and facility and system access for terminated employees.

■ Have an employee identification system in place for positive identification and access control purposes. Employees should only be given access to those secure areas needed for the performance of their duties. Company management needs to adequately control the issuance of identification badges.

■ Procedures must be in place to identify, challenge, and address unauthorized/unidentified persons who enter the property.

- Provide employee orientation that includes security awareness and loss prevention initiatives.
- Establish a company reward and tip hotline to provide employees and others with incentives and venues in which to report security or policy related violations (J. Coughlin 2010).

This is true for just about any company in any industry, but it is especially important in the supply chain for service providers. In my career conducting investigations and now assisting companies with their security, one of the big issues I see is hiring employees with criminal pasts. It would be real nice if we could all sing "Kumbayah" and give people second chances in our industry, but it does not seem to work out. Companies I worked for had hiring guidelines and did background screenings, but quite often when I was doing internal investigations, I would find that the suspected employee did, in fact, have a history that should have prevented his employment. On several occasions that missed background was a major factor in pointing out the suspect or solidifying the evidence. If you are going to entrust a driver with thousands of dollars worth of high value freight, you best be able to trust him. Here is another quote for which I can't give proper credit to the originator, but it is very true and seldom wrong: "The best indicator of future behavior is the past."

Due to the way that public background searches work and the information they rely upon being only official convictions, it leaves most of those services in the lurch. If you are involved in doing a company investigation and the police become involved, have them run a background screening through their law enforcement system because they can get information of past arrests and other details not based on convictions. I tell people all of the time that in Texas you could probably have quite a few arrests for theft offenses and never have a conviction due to the system of using non-adjudicated probations and other courthouse stalls, especially in the large metropolitan counties. This has been such a problem that it made me seek a way to design a background screening program for Transportation. I worked with another former police officer, Kevin Heath, who has a company, C-Net Technologies, which does background screening and vendor management. We put together a very comprehensive background screening program for these people that enables screenings to find the data you are seeking because it focuses on the county level with actual physical checks of those records.

Bad or unsuitable drivers are a cause for many problems and proper screening is important. In almost every case where I worked a theft-related investigation involving an employee, either through my own searching or through the involved law enforcement agency, we were able to find history which confirmed the behavior of the suspect being investigated. Do not be fooled by cheap database checks, they do not protect you and are not worth the money you think you are saving. One bad employee can cost you a large amount of money. We were recently contacted by a SWTSC company that had an employee who stole more than $250K, including fuel, vehicle parts, and client freight. When the employee involvement came to light, law enforcement agents discovered he had numerous felony convictions, which the company's background screening program had not revealed. That company could have done a lot of good backgrounds with that $250K. Instead it was out that money because management wanted to save a few bucks and used an incomplete, unproven service. Proper background screening may cost more upfront, but it will save a bunch down the line.

The other main factor that ensures personnel security is training and orientation. A company culture of safety and security should be promoted from the very start. Discuss company security expectations as part of the orientation so employees know it is a prerogative.

Facility Physical Security

Companies should have:

- Access controls to prevent unauthorized entry to facilities, maintain control of employees and visitors and protect company assets. Access controls must include the positive identification of all employees, visitors, and vendors at all points of entry.
- Visitors must present photo identification for documentation purposes upon arrival. All visitors should be escorted and visibly display temporary identification.
- Proper vendor ID and/or photo identification must be presented for documentation purposes upon arrival by all vendors. Arriving packages and mail should be periodically screened before being disseminated.
- A search policy making all persons and vehicles entering or leaving company facilities subject to search with signs posted with such language at all major points of access and egress.
- All fencing must be regularly inspected for integrity and damage. The fencing should be of adequate material to form a physical barrier barring easy entry or access.
- No Trespass signs posted on perimeter of facility and fences to enforce laws as applicable to local and state statutes.
- Facilities with alarm protection including redundant wireless verified alarm system back-up if location stores high value goods to monitor premises and prevent unauthorized access to cargo handling and storage areas.
- Segregated high value secure storage areas if location stores high value goods or controlled substances.
- Adequate lighting must be provided inside and outside the facility including the following areas: entrances and exits, cargo handling, storage areas, fence lines, and parking areas.

- All external and internal windows, gates and fences must be secured with locking devices. Management or security personnel must control the issuance of all locks and keys, to include the locks and keys for tractors. When parked in the yard, doors to tractors and trailers should be closed.
- Private passenger vehicles must be prohibited from parking in close proximity to the storage areas for tractors and trailers and should be segregated by fencing if possible.
- Gates through which all vehicles and/or personnel enter or exit should be manned and/or monitored. The number of gates should be kept to the minimum necessary for proper access and safety.
- Any vehicle entering the yard should have license plate, model and driver's information recorded. (J. Coughlin 2010)

Controlling the premises where you conduct business is paramount to security and control. The listed facility recommendations are for large metropolitan business units and each bullet point should be reviewed for each separate unit and those which are applicable to that unit's operation should be put in place. Probably the most important recommendation for each location is the need for good lighting. Criminals do not like well-lit yards and areas. So, no matter the size of the facility or yard, make the lighting your first consideration because it is an extremely effective deterrent. There are also very good products to consider in this section of your security plan. If you are experiencing security breaches from external sources through fencing, add an electric fence to that yard and the problem will be resolved. When I was working in the industry and had facilities in five states, I added an electric fence to the ones where I had multiple break-ins or fence cuttings leading to trailer shopping and theft of propane tanks or other items and brought those activities to a complete halt. I recommend a product such as Electric Guard Dog because it is inexpensive, attaches to the current fence, and is easy to look at while being wonderfully effective. The other technology I recommend is a verified video alarm system such as Videofied. This is a stand-alone system. It is not integrated into the main alarm and control panel and will protect your business from the high value business burglars who beat your alarm using the different techniques we talked about earlier. If the burglar does manage to beat your alarm, this technology will catch him and send a verifying video of the intruder to the police. This will cause them to respond, especially if they have already quit responding because they believe the alarm is dysfunctional.

If you have to use a guard service to protect your facility or property, be sure to vet them properly and do not hire based only on the cost factor. Never sign the guard company's general contract. Have a guard company representative sign your contract prepared with the services and requirements you set out. Also prepare the guard post orders with the services you want performed and the information you require them to capture. One of the biggest problems with contracted guards, is their under use and general lack of expectations. You pay good money for their services so make the contracted guards a part of the team. If you give them responsibilities, it actually makes them feel like more of a member of the operation and they can become a contributing force instead of a non-contributing placeholder.

Business Partner Requirements

Companies you partner with should:

■ Have written and verifiable processes for the screening of business partners including carrier's agents, subcontracted highway carriers, and service providers as well as screening procedures for new customers, beyond financial soundness issues to include security indicators, such as business references and professional associations.

■ Have mutual written security standards equivalent to your own company requirements and guidelines which can be contractually enforced (security contract addendums available).

■ As highway carriers have the ultimate responsibility for all cargo loaded aboard their trailer or conveyance, they must communicate the importance of supply chain security.

■ Have a security contact/group responsible for the written security processes.

■ Report all major losses or thefts to your company immediately.

■ Partner with you during the recovery of a loss.

■ Conduct loss reviews and corrective action plans on all major losses.

■ Allow your company to audit all phases of the contractual agreement.

■ Participate in regional industry councils and industry-wide information sharing programs. (J. Coughlin 2010)

Proper relationships between partners are often overlooked and not controlled as closely as they should be. One of the big problems in relationships between shippers and carriers is that they are immediately put at odds by the carrier claims process, especially if the claims amount has the potential to be greater if the carrier was negligent or had some fault in the loss. This wedge between companies sometimes makes it harder for them to work together when there is a major issue.

When a major loss occurs, it is of tantamount importance to have all parties on deck reach into their bags of contacts and resources to work together to make the best effort at recovery. By holding a loss from the shipper while the carrier tries to determine the circumstances and make the recovery, the whole recovery process and effort is hampered. Be true partners when the chips are down, and you will have a much better relationship and working partnership every time.

As far as vendors who come on your property to conduct business are concerned, have a vendor management system in place to vet them and their employees to your guidelines and standards and place them in an audit process to make sure they remain contractually fit. I have seen a multitude of problems result from undervetted vendor companies wherein their employees gain access to your business areas, but do not match your company's business security and hiring qualifications. It is important to have a standardized partnership requirement across the entire company so that one terminal is not doing it one way and another is doing it another. Company partnerships are crucial to the success of the company and should be entered into with viable relationships and expectations.

Procedural Security

Companies should have:

- Security measures in place to ensure the integrity and security of processes relevant to the transportation, handling, and storage of cargo in the supply chain to prevent, detect, or deter un-manifested material from gaining access onto the commercial conveyance.
- Procedures in place that document the movement, handling, and storage of cargo in the supply chain.
- A manifesting system in place which will ensure the integrity of the cargo and be accurate, timely and able to be archived.
- A manifesting system which accurately described, weighed, labeled, marked, counted, and verified each shipment. Departing cargo should be checked against purchase or delivery orders. Drivers involved in the delivering, receiving, or handling of cargo must be positively identified during the shipment process.
- All shortages, overages, and other significant discrepancies or anomalies must be resolved and/or investigated appropriately. The appropriate law enforcement agencies

should be notified if illegal or suspicious activities are detected.

■ Cargo properly marked and manifested to include accurate weight and piece count.

■ A process in place where all vehicle identification information (unit numbers, license plate and state and VIN) of the involved carriers equipment is recorded and easily accessible when needed.

■ A documented theft recovery plan. (J. Coughlin 2010)

All of the above is pretty normal for most transportation and logistics companies with the exception of a written theft recovery plan. If a company has a security manager or group, the theft recovery plan is usually to call security. The plan needs to be much more specific and include the ability to immediately provide law enforcement officers with the information to make their police reports. They will need the license plate numbers and VIN numbers of the involved vehicle/equipment. They will need a good description of the involved cargo and the ability to quickly obtain any related serial numbers. They will need pertinent driver information in case the driver is not available. Remember, the opportunity to recover the cargo is about a sixteen-hour window in the best case scenario. Any delay in getting this information into the hands of law enforcement reduces the chances of recovery. You also must have the ability to get a BOLO/Alert out through the industry sources as quickly as possible. Not having or doing the above will impede your chances of recovery every time. Be prepared. Know who you are going to call and what you need as soon as you get the bad news. At the Southwest Transportation Security Council we have a Cargo Theft Reporting Template. If we receive the information in this format, we can send it to our contacts, including state police agencies near the offense location and that information will be sent to the road vehicles in short order. Here is the template the SWTSC uses:

CARGO THEFT REPORT

Stolen Trailer: Give trailer description (make and
model) including color and markings:
License Plate number and State:
VIN Number:

Tractor:
Give Tractor make and model description including
color and markings
License number and State:
VIN Number

Stolen from:
Give location including address, city, and state

Date and Time:
Give date and time of incident or range of dates and
times

Stolen Cargo:
Describe missing freight
Commodity/Amount/Description

Police report number and Agency:
Give police agency taking report or handling the
incident

Police Contact Info:
Give agency contact information to include any officer names and phone number

Reporting Person:
If different from police/company reporting person

Reporting Person contact information:
Reporting Person's phone number/email address

Further info:
Give brief narrative of how incident occurred

Source: J. Coughlin, 2009.

In-Transit Security

Companies should:

- Have security measures for the company assets, freight, and drivers during in-transit moves.
- Have drivers perform a documented equipment checklist and inspection of unit prior to departure including documentation of seal number and verification of being properly applied.
- Processes in place to monitor the movement of the company units in-transit and have the ability to communicate with the drivers at all time.
- Perform a documented, periodic, and unannounced verification process to ensure the logs are maintained and company tracking and monitoring procedures are being followed and enforced.
- Have seal verification processes in place at all locations to check departing and arriving trailers. All empty trailers being removed from a location should have the inside of the trailer physically checked to prevent the removal of unauthorized property from that location.
- Have a process in place for the discovery of a broken seal during the in-transit move and its documentation as to when discovered, how it was broken, and to whom it was reported.
- Use satellite tracking technology on the tractor and trailer equipment and use covert cargo tracking in the freight if load has a high value and is a known targeted commodity of organized cargo thieves.
- Provide drivers with locks and immobilization devices.
- Plan routes to avoid high crime areas and known problem truck stops and drop areas.
- Provide drivers with security awareness training to include information on what steps they should take if

they believe they are being followed especially if they have come from an origin of a high value shipper's location.
■ Have a recovery plan in place in the case of any reported loss.

Drivers should:

■ Start with full fuel tanks from origin pick up.
■ Have the DOT hours to complete the pull or to travel for a long period before having to stop.
■ Avoid unnecessary stops.
■ Always keep equipment locked and use immobilization devices when leaving the equipment unattended.
■ Only stop in well-lighted, secure areas.
■ Never leave the loaded rig or trailer unattended in an unsecured location.
■ Always notify dispatch or employer of route change due to weather or other problems.
■ When doing LTL pick-up and delivery, use high quality locks on the doors at all times, especially when having to leave the units unattended. (J. Coughlin 2010)

For shippers and carriers, this section is very pertinent so we will discuss it at length. The hardest part of this policy is getting the driver or drivers to follow all of your guidelines or regulations. Drivers tend to become the kings of their own worlds once they take to the road. It is important to impress on them the importance of taking care of this high value load. It is very important for the drivers to follow the guidelines and not deviate from the security plan. Most importantly, drivers must understand the risks and the methods that thieves will use to take the rig and load from them. Making them aware is the most important part of this section. The drivers have no chance of recognizing a problem or understanding the risk if they are not made aware of the risk inherent with the high value load and the methods of operation used by organized cargo criminals. Drivers should be given a driver awareness warning sheet containing information that will remind them of their responsibilities, explain what they should be on the look-out for and providing a number to respond to should they have a problem. The drivers should be given a driver warning sheet and be briefed on the issue during the pick-up process at origin. On the next page is a Driver Warning Sheet template that I have provided to customers and colleagues.

Giving the driver or drivers this sheet during a briefing puts them on notice that this load is high value and has been a target of organized criminals in the past. It gives drivers a way to respond should they see something suspicious and it also reinforces the high value handling procedures that are involved in this move. Many times drivers are required to sign for this sheet during the briefing which makes their responsibility for this load very plain. Driver actions are normally the weak point in any in-transit security plan. Remember from the charts about location of thefts and the description of the organized thieves' methods of operation that the targeted load becomes an opportunity when left unattended. It does not matter where the load is left or for how long, thieves are looking for the opening. The drivers must not give it to them. Drivers should be expected to provide the protection of the units if they have been given the knowledge, awareness and way to respond.

Many high value shippers now have programs in place that contractually require the carriers to arrive to origin with full fuel tanks, enough hours of service for driver to service the requirement of traveling at least a minimum of 200 miles from the origin before stopping. These requirements are put in place to make it more difficult for the possible suspects who may follow the units from the location.

When we first started using covert cargo AGPS devices in the cargo, they were placed as security devices for the freight. An advantage in using the devices was that they provided the shipper with visibility of the shipment from origin to

ATTENTION DRIVERS!

Individuals will follow you with the intent to steal your entire truck and trailer if left unattended or unsecured.

Immediately notify local law enforcement authorities and your dispatch if you believe you are being followed.

Follow your company guidelines for in-transit high value freight handling.

(1) Always engage any issued anti-theft and immobilization devices and remove the keys from your tractor, including spare keys, when leaving the truck during breaks or fuel stops. Lock all windows and doors.

(2) Never leave your truck engine running while away from the truck.

(3) If you're part of a driver team, one of you must stay with the load at all times.

(4) If you must stop for a break, park in a manner to ensure a full view of your load at all times and inspect seals before leaving and upon return.

(5) Do not discuss the contents of your load with anyone.

We strongly advise against stopping for any reason if load cannot be attended, secured or kept in sight at all times!

If your load is stolen, immediately notify law enforcement, your dispatch and _____ at _____ 24 hours a day.

Source: J. Coughlin, Driver Warning Sheet 2001.

destination and recorded the actions and activities of the carrier. This tool became a great auditing process and evaluator of carriers for the shippers. The shippers now had more information and with the use of virtual fencing and alert notification, they could control the carriers' behaviors and monitor activities better than ever before. Shippers were now able to enforce those contractual requirements they put in place for the carriers because of the visibility of the shipment the AGPS gives them.

The last bullet in the above list of in-transit security needs is to have a recovery plan in place in the case of any reported loss. This is very important and fundamental. Earlier in the book, I spoke about a sixteen-hour rule concerning the opportunity to recover the cargo from an in-transit theft. This means that you must be prepared the moment you receive the call that a theft has occurred. This preparation includes having the equipment information, at minimum the license plate/state of the of the involved tractor; the license plate/state of the trailer; the commodity information of the cargo and the identification information, including the CDL of the driver, in case he is also missing. This now gives you the information so that a police report can be made at the original jurisdiction which enables that agency to put that information in the National Crime Information Computer (NCIC). This is important because entering the information in the NCIC allows other agencies to check the license plate and get a stolen verification.

Your recovery plan should also include preparing a cargo theft reporting template and forwarding the report to your local council or to one of the regional councils for dissemination through the BOLO/Alert notification systems they operate with industry and law enforcement contacts. Your recovery plan should include notifying all parties of the shipment including the shipper and insurer so they can bring to bear all of their law enforcement contacts and get all hands on deck. When a major theft occurs, this is not the time to withhold information from any of the parties; it is the time to engage all resources. If the cargo is not found but the empty equipment is located, make sure law enforcement, an SIU insurance investigator, or a private investigator is dispatched to the scene to follow-up on possible leads in that area including checking for surveillance cameras from businesses in the area or known operations or related offense location information from previous incidents. If the cargo is not recovered and a criminal investigation does not lead to a prosecution but does identify possible suspects, companies should look at the possibility of a civil prosecution against the higher level criminal actors based on a preponderance of evidence. Many of the higher level buyers and participants have assets, and filing a civil suit may be worth the effort based on the evidence or information that has been found. If the company legal staff does not have that expertise, a transportation attorney or law firm could be retained to pursue those possibilities. These types of legal actions can severely hamper and impede the financial parties behind the thefts.

The recovery plan involves operating in a manner that prepares you for the worst and when something occurs, not making it worse. Most of this is simple and elementary, but you would be surprised by the number of operations that let trucks bump their docks and take the freight without recording any of the driver or equipment particulars. That makes it worse. Although much of this in-transit security is directed at FTL operations, the last bullet for the driver is related to LTL operations and it states that when doing LTL pick-up and delivery, high quality locks should be used on the doors at all times, especially when having to leave the units unattended. The company I worked for had two LTL companies. The pick-up and delivery (P&D) drivers were issued locks for their units just for this purpose. It was in their standard operating procedures and these were reinforced constantly. Just as over the road drivers are kings of their own world, so apparently are the P&D runners. When I was a security manager, we had numerous incidents where following this simple rule would have prevented the problem, but drivers would start the day with the lock in place. Then, after the first stop, the driver would lock the lock to the door handle and go about their duties during their city operation, leaving the truck contents vulnerable to quick attacks by opportunistic thieves. Auditing and monitoring the enforcement of this locking rule is well worthwhile.

Information Technology Security

Companies should:

- Protect data from unauthorized access or manipulation.
- Establish and review access levels for operation person-nel establishing a "need to know" rule for the shipping information.
- Have a system in place that is password protected which could identify the abuse of IT including improper access, tampering or the altering of business data. (J. Coughlin 2010)

I do not proclaim myself an expert in the IT field, just the opposite. I do know that access to the shipping and loading information needs to be held at a level where not everyone on the dock can have vision of all shipping or storage records. Many times, when a trailer is stolen from a yard or is broken into on the yard, there is the possibility of collusion or col-laboration from the inside. From the investigative standpoint, it is not too hard to tell if the criminals knew what they were looking for. If you have ten trailers on the ready line and the criminals cut through a fence and go directly to one unit leav-ing the others unmolested, they probably had inside infor-mation. So the question is who had the information of the shipments which were loaded on that unit and how did they know? It may have nothing at all to do with IT access, but it very well could. Establishing access to the shipping and load-ing information on a need-to-know basis is just good business and eliminates multiple sources of potential issues.

Brokerage and Freight Boards

Shippers and carriers using brokerage, sub-contractors, or posting loads to freight boards should be aware of the risk of company identity theft and fraudulent or fictitious pick-ups.

If using these services, the broker agent should:

- Confirm that the company that they are doing business with is legitimate and has a good track record of performance. Use a carrier management system or carrier selection process to vet your carriers.
- Obtain references and call organizations to verify past performance.
- Contact the Better Business Bureau in the shipper's area to see if any complaints have been lodged against the provider.
- Access www.safersys.org to validate company, DOT number, insurance and registration.
- Contact company to confirm pick up information and insurer and current insurance.
- Confirm listed business/operating location of the involved carrier.
- Do not provide information or fax application to phone numbers which you can't confirm to original company information.
- Place a higher scrutiny on operations using a 714 or 786 phone area code.

When driver and equipment arrives on-site shipper should:

- Cross reference name with identification and ensure that driver's handwriting is legible on documents he signs and matches signature on his driver's license.
- Document and photocopy all information on CDL including state and obtain thumb print of the driver.
- Document particulars about the transport vehicles, including license plate number and state.
- Take picture of tractor and trailer or at a minimum note markings and identifiers on both units. (J. Coughlin 2010)

With the fraudulent pick-ups and fictitious company identity theft, brokerage and Internet freight boards offer much opportunity for illegal activity. Even though this is a somewhat new phenomenon, we have collected enough data to start putting a finger on how they operate, what they target and who they are, which gives us an idea as to what needs to be done to eliminate the current opportunities to commit fraud. We have already discussed their methods of operation earlier in the book so we know they operate illegally in several different ways. The first is to create a company based on the identity theft of a person's name. When this is done, everything is set up making the company look legitimate. Flags to look for include the time of the insurance policy was put in place and the operating location. Several investigations have shown us that the operating locations are often mailbox rental locations. So, if you have a question, Google the location and see if you can determine whether it is a truck terminal or an appropriate business or have a site inspection preformed as part of the vetting.

In the other scenario, thieves steal the identity of a legitimate carrier and bid on loads using that carrier's information. Often they change the company contact information or ask the broker to fax the application to a non-company fax number. This can usually be vetted via a check of the legitimate company's website. Also, since many involved in this scam are of Armenian descent, one should be suspicious if the caller has an eastern European accent and a 714 area code, since many of these criminals seem to work from the North Hollywood, California, or a 786 area code as some South Floridians have adopted this scam. To protect one's company from these predators, you must understand the current weaknesses in the carrier selection process and, based on the awareness of the current trends, take the vetting process steps further when necessary. It is also important to share information so that during pick-up, if suspicions are raised there can be communication between both the shippers and brokers and a process to not accept the selected carrier. Networking, communication, and information sharing have never been more important.

Security Training and Threat Awareness

Security training and awareness should be incorporated into each company's culture starting with employee orientation. The program should foster security awareness and reinforce the importance of security to the company operation.

Employees should be trained to report suspicious activities including theft, the introduction of contraband into the system, and any activity involving business abuse. Additionally, specific training should be offered to assist employees in maintaining trailer and tractor integrity, recognizing internal conspiracies, in-transit vulnerabilities and dangers, and protecting company access controls including confronting unauthorized persons on company property. These programs should offer incentives (reward/TIP program) for active employee participation. (J. Coughlin 2010)

I know I have harped on this continually throughout this book, but it is one, if not the most important parts of any transportation and logistics company program. Awareness of the threats and risks make employees much more cognizant of things going on around them. Reinforcing security, just like safety, makes for a better work environment and allows employees to know the importance the company places on the issue. Having a reward program and a security hotline let employees know that the company takes it serious. If you have a hot-line, make sure you send the hotline reward information to each employees' residence or publish it in a newsletter. The spouses or romantic interests of employees have provided me much information in the past about an employee's job-related honesty when their relationship sometimes go sour. This provides more information than you may realize.

Legal Best Practices

Companies should:

- Have corporate counsel or hire specific transportation counsel who know the legal doctrine of Transportation law including:
  1. Hague Convention-International Agreements
  2. Hague Visby
  3. COGSA (Carrier of Goods Sea Act)
  4. Warsaw Convention-Air Cargo
  5. Rotterdam-Contract Out or Designate International Standard as to limit of Liability
  6. Carmack-U.S. Federal Interstate Cargo Laws
- Prepare contracts specific to the needs of their specific company, operation and security requirements for each provider including:
  1. Shipper/Carrier
  2. Brokers
  3. Depot, Terminal or Container, Trailer or Drop Yards
  4. Security Service Providers
  5. Vendors
  6. Personnel/Temp Employee Providers (J. Coughlin 2010)

This part of the SWTSC Best Practices was prepared with the assistance from our council transportation attorney, Mr. Steve Lewis, Esquire. It is important to understand and be able to operate within the correct legislative influence. Having an attorney who understand the laws and can correctly interpret them when necessary is very useful. Steve has been a great addition to the SWTSC membership and a guiding light for our nonprofit entity along with educational instruction and taking care of the council's legal responsibilities with subpoenas and such. One of the things I recommend in most circumstances is to not use a service provider's contract, at least not without review. Most of those are slanted toward the provider and do not give the involved company the latitude to audit and evaluate the provider's service. It is important to prepare contracts for all of the above listed providers specifically for their service with your company. This allows setting the contract standard for the service along with the guidelines and the auditing of those guidelines laid out in common terms. I believe all vendors and service providers should be subject to audit and review to confirm that they are following the contractual guidelines. When I was working in the transportation industry, we had several logistics and warehouse circumstances where we used temp agencies to provide part-time employees. We set the guidelines for those employees as far as background and drug screening and then an auditing process whereby the temp agency provided documentation to confirm the screening had been completed for any employee who was assigned to our account. Because of co-employment issues and the law, this can be a problem if it is not dealt with contractually and legally. Each contract for services has specific requirements you want to set and then audit for confirmation and evaluation. Security guard contracts and post orders should definitely be prepared by the hiring entity and not the provider.

Current Technologies for Prevention and Recovery

There are many products in the market for cargo theft prevention and protection. There are locks, king pin locks, immobilization devices, and many other products which provide many different deterrents. The largest problem with most of them is that they have to be applied by the drivers. This has been a huge issue in the past as drivers, once on the road, tend to have an aversion to applying security devices each and every time when they leave the loaded vehicle unattended. We have seen from the past discussion that the thieves are able to steal a complete rig most of the time in less than ninety seconds and are just looking for that unattended vehicle opportunity. Over a period of time, I have seen the industry moving toward security which is covert and can be applied or monitored remotely. This takes away the total dependence on a driver.

Back in the days when technology wasn't available to provide immediate access to information, supply chain security was limited to physical obstacles such as fences, locks, seals, and uniformed guards. There were also closed loop camera surveillance systems with video recorders which were set up to oversee warehouse and transportation facilities usually with limitations in the recording capabilities and reproduction. These all had a significant impact on facilities but did little or nothing for the security of loads while in-transit. These loads were subject to theft by thieves having only a bolt cutter, crow bar or ignition puller. Most of the times, the drivers and carriers had no real awareness of the risks and threats. The shippers were also in the dark about the problem until they were victimized. I know when the company I worked for had our 3PL take over an account of a large computer manufacturer; our company started operating the warehousing and distribution without a single word about the issue. It was not until we started to experience Full Truckload losses did our investigators began to gather intelligence and information to identify the root cause of the thefts. It was the organized South Florida crews who were at work and our assigned security personnel had to discover their methods of operation from real world losses. Over a period of time, our company investigators had a list of over two hundred fifty (250) crew members who were persons of interest in losses from our 3PL location. The security personnel put together some driver awareness programs and worked closely with the carrier security teams. Large company carriers were hired, as they had better systems and security groups to respond to the threats and risks. At this time the embedded cargo security AGPS was not really available in the market but the need for full visibility of shipments from origin to destinations was shown to be sorely needed.

Most carriers had fleet management systems based on GPS. These systems focused on operations and maximizing equipment usage but did not protect the cargo at all. In matter of fact, the organized criminals were known to immediately disable the fleet management GPS systems upon the theft of the vehicle. The only record you would have from these systems was a last ping identifying when and where the theft occurred.

As mobile communications, technology and web-based solutions came on the scene in the supply chain, companies started providing the AGPS tracking to offer a truly integrated solution for in-transit protection. The solution included the use of embedded cargo AGPS devices. The program included the use of the covert tracking, along with monitoring, controlling the shipment's carrier, and providing recovery, investigation and prevention.

Covert tracking stepped up the security game against the South Florida crew method of operation. This covert application did not allow the criminals to disconnect the tracking device and would not allow them the time to search for the device and locate it prior to the police being able to respond. It has made them change their method of operations but has not stopped their activity. The monitoring, using virtual geo-fencing available on the mapping and tracking interfaces, allow the shippers to have vision of their shipment from origin to destination. It allows them to monitor the carrier and control the shipment movement. The system can alert to many circumstances, including exit and entry of geo-fence locations and routes, stationary and moving after stationary, and protocols can be set by the shipper with requirements put in place for their designated carrier. The monitoring is conducted to confirm the carrier is following the set out requirements. The monitoring also allows for recovery in the case of a theft or problem. The recovery is made by vectoring law enforcement to the stolen unit once the determination of theft is made. It does not do any good to track something if upon receiving an exception, you can't respond and recover. This not as easy as it may sound, but the main companies that offer this service have very robust recovery capabilities.

The monitoring and subsequent shipment history of each move can also be used by the shipper to evaluate the carrier's performance during their overall annual business review.

When you talk about investigation, the transmissions you get from the unit will provide location based investigative information. Using this documented information, industry security managers and law enforcement can locate and identify locations the criminal element operate and use for their illegal activities. This intelligence is very important for follow-up and piecing together larger conspiracies, related offenses, and long-term organized crime cases along with fencing locations, safe houses, and storage operations.

GPS, Assisted GPS, Cellular (CDMA and GSM), and integration with Radio Frequency provides a multi-faceted solution that can integrate the right solution for a shipper based on needs and coverage, to deliver the most advanced features available for covert protection and tracking, real-time surveillance and web-based monitoring along with integration with law enforcement for dispatch and recovery. A truck owner can also use an RF vehicle recovery system as an added layer of protection for trucks and trailers. Since most thefts occur while the driver is out of the truck at an unsecured location, having a tracking device hidden in the cargo as well as on the truck and trailer, gives the driver the freedom to stop at a rest area or truck stop knowing that his entire rig is protected without having to turn on a single switch or apply a single device. This type of technology, which can monitor and react remotely, is the future of the transportation security industry.

Most companies have figured out that they need to remove the human factor from the equation as much as possible. The use of web-based monitoring and mobile communication is the impending wave of future products as most security providers are looking for better ways to protect or immobilize the truck and trailer without having to depend on the driver.

Covert AGPS systems and mobile communication locking or controlling devices which can be monitored or applied remotely is where the security for the in-transit piece of the transportation industry is heading, especially for high value shipments. In the not too distant future, insurers are going to require this type of technology in return for affordable high value cargo shipment liability insurance coverage.

Old fashioned hardware locks still provide a certain aspect of security and continue to have their place in the industry but it is time to step up the transportation security game. During the theft of a chassis and container reported to the SWTSC recently, the complainant had a video camera at the gate of the involved yard. The camera caught the image of the criminals entering the yard in their tractor and removing a chassis and container, all within two minutes. The complainant stated that the chassis had been secured in the yard with a king pin lock. So it took the thieves less than two minutes to enter the yard, break off the king pin lock, hook the chassis and drive away. This freight was never recovered. Within five minutes, the thieves returned and took a second unit, also in less than two minutes. The broken king pin locks were found on the ground.

Had these same units been tracked and geo-fenced, when they left the location they would have alerted their owners or monitors and the units could have been tracked to a location where the police could have responded. Going with the new technology is the future and the industry is slowly trending in that direction. The Internet and technology have changed everything and transportation security is no different, even though it is transforming at a very leisurely pace.

There are many different products and technologies which are available today and which continue to grow cheaper and better with the evolution of systems. Photos can be taken of units, drivers, and drivers' licenses. Units can be fitted with remote locking technology, tracking and immobilization devices, and when layered with old fashioned locking and RF recovery devices the units begin to have the security that is needed for high value shipping. Technology is now available to specifically track air shipments and ocean and rail containers via GPS technology. Some of the technology is still a little expensive but will slowly depreciate with time and further invention, interaction, and use. Even though technology provides many new robust products with tremendous capabilities, all are not 100% fail safe. You still need layered protection and very adroit procedures and protocols.

When looking at new technology for facilities, I want to point out the wireless verified video alarm units such as "Videofied." This is a solution to the South Floridian warehouse burglary method of operation. Remember earlier when we discussed their methods of operations where they both steal the code through surreptitious activities or eventually break-in and cut the power to the complete integrated security system and control panel after setting off the alarm numerous times making it appear the alarm is faulty. Once they gain entry and law enforcement and the stakeholders quit responding, they use the warehouse equipment to stage the freight for loading into trailers to complete their theft unless the warehouse has a wireless verified video alarm unit. This unit, powered by its own battery and wireless communication, takes a ten (10) second video clip based on motion. That video clip is sent to a monitoring center who determines that the motion is caused by the burglars. The clip is sent on to the police showing them that the alarm location is in fact under siege by thieves and it was not a false alarm. With this new information, they respond promptly to a burglary in progress. This type of alarm can be used for many purposes, outside

AN EXAMPLE OF LAYERED SECURITIES

Recently, at the company where I work, we were tracking some very high value shipments going from a Mexico origin to a Canadian destination for a large consumer product company. For this tracking application, we use an AGPS GSM tracking base unit with 20AH of battery and layered with an RF beacon technology. When the driver arrived at the destination location in Canada in the early morning hours, he was inside the virtual geo-fence but not inside the receiving location's physical barrier. His arrival in the virtual geo-fence set the tracking device to a longer reporting rate. Waiting to make the delivery, the driver climbed into his sleeper to await the morning receiving shift. After a short period of time, he heard the tractor window break and was confronted by two gunmen who had him disable an immobilization device, tied him up, and placed him back in the sleeper area of the tractor. The suspects drove the unit for about forty (40) minutes and bumped a dock. The driver could feel and hear them off-loading his trailer. When they finished, they drove him about fifteen (15) minutes away and abandoned the unit and him. Once he was able to untie himself, he notified the authorities. When the monitoring center was notified, they could not get the tracking device to provide a cellular or GPS signal. Authorities who had been notified were put in touch with our Canadian company members and a RF receiver was provided and tuned to the advised RF frequency. When law enforcement checked several locations where these types of cargo criminals were known to operate, they were able to vector into the beacon signal with the RF receiver at a warehouse complex. Law enforcement put the location under surveillance, used the RF tracking information to obtain a search warrant and then when they saw activity at the location, they executed the search warrant. Inside they found the involved freight from our customer's theft and over $500K of merchandise from other cargo crimes. They also made eight arrests. The interesting fact was when the freight was found, the criminals had placed a cellular jamming device on top of the freight, which was prohibiting the AGPS device from transmitting. The jamming device did not jam the RF signal; it actually enhanced that signal allowing the eventual recovery. This is an example of using layered security and multiple recovery capabilities.

copper thefts, construction yards, and remote locations but it is the currently a proven solution to the professional burglars who target high value warehouses.

There are many technologies and solutions for commercial issues. Name the problem and find a solution. The majority of the time the answer does not have to cost a lot of money. One of the best solutions out there is older but is tried and true. That is electric fencing for yards where external theft becomes a huge problem. During my time in the industry, I put that solution in four (4) locations. Each and every time I went from having numerous breaches a week to absolutely nothing. The

Figure 6.1 This sign, whether power is engaged or not, acts as a good deterrent by providing perimeter control to prevent illegal entry.

Electric Guard Dog product is one of my personal favorites. The barrier works by the sign alone, and on several occasions I have known it to do so because some governmental zoning issues have forced companies to turn them off.

The fence is really not noticeable and is surely not an eyesore, health hazard or a risk. It works using:

- 7,000 Volt Electrical PULSE—every 1.3 seconds
- Extremely SHORT—.0001 to .0004 seconds—pulsed versus steady power
- Therefore, poses NO medical risk … yet strong enough to zap intruders off or away from fence
- 10-foot tall (approx), 20-strand Electric Fence
- Energized by 12-volt marine battery
- Charged by a solar panel. (Allows remote installation. Eliminates daily energy costs.)
- Safety of The Electric Guard Dog is certified—well below international standards established by IEC 60335-2-76

I used this solution and know many others who have also used it. It is the real deal with positive results. In one location where I had it installed, I was able to do away with one 24/7 guard, which allowed me to pay for the fence and have budget money left over. Very reasonable solution with great results!!

Cargo Insurance

Cargo insurance coverage does not come standard with your commercial trucking insurance policy, and the purchase of a full coverage vehicle policy does not cover your freight if it is damaged or stolen. Cargo insurance is a separate policy, which covers the freight you are hauling if lost, damaged, or stolen. Considering that many loads that are worth thousands of dollars, you can understand why this coverage is so important and required by many contracts to protect their property while it is in the care, custody, and control of the carrier. Many companies are self-insured up to certain thresholds, and if they suffer a loss or damage, they pay that amount directly from their own funds. It is extremely important to make certain that the cargo insurance being used does not have exclusions from covering the necessary risks and is in the appropriate amounts. Cargo insurance policies many times come with some built in coverage. Make sure you understand what is covered and what is excluded. Not having the proper cargo insurance coverage can leave you paying some large off the bottom line costs if something unexpected happens.

I spoke with Mr. Vance Root, a Vice-President at U.S. Risk about current Cargo insurance policies. He referred me to some cargo related information articles in the *Insurance Journal* which had the following quote. "The global commercial property insurance market is continuing to show signs of upwards rate trends, especially for catastrophe-exposed risks," said Dean Klisura, U.S. Risk Practices Leader, and Marsh.

Klisura said that the U.S. property market continues to be in a state of transition with insureds more likely to experience rate increases than those renewing with flat or modest rate decreases. "We believe that this trend will continue in the short term, with the average rate of increase continuing to rise month over month," the Marsh executive said (Marsh 2012).

So cargo insurance rates are subject to the upward pressures according to the insurance professionals but not any way out of the norm of the current market.

Let's look at the different Cargo Insurance definitions as provided by U.S. Risk.

Motor Truck Cargo—This type of insurance protects the owner or the carrier against certain types of perils like theft, damage during transit, and various other occurrences that cause loss depending on the type of cargo being shipped. Mostly all of the products that are shipped over land can and should be insured for a specific coverage under a motor truck cargo insurance policy.

Marine Cargo—This type of insurance protects cargo being shipped internationally, usually by sea or air. This also protects the owner or the carrier in the event of a loss due to damage or exposure to weather, jettison, theft, mishandling or damage from the loading and the unloading process. Other special circumstances can also be insured like a breakdown in equipment, i.e., refrigeration units, or delays that expose perishable items.

Open Cargo Policies—This type of insurance is usually for carriers or owners that would involve coverage for large volumes of cargo. There are many types of policies that have broad coverage for many areas of truck and marine cargo insurance; one of the most common is an open perils policy, or open cargo policy. Any party with a vested interest can insure a certain agreed value or a specified period of time or both. These policies are broad in nature and do not usually list the details of the specific transaction such as the name of the ship, destination or specific details of the cargo being insured since it is an agreed value or time that is being insured.

Voyage Policies—This type of insurance is to insure that the cargo gets from its place of origin to its final destination. This type of policy has more specific details than an open cargo policy since the terms are for a certain trip with a specific origination to a destination at a specified location. Because there are many types of potential delays, the length of the passage is not typically stated. After the cargo has been delivered to the specified destination, then the cargo the policy would typically expire and a new policy would have to be written to continue coverage to the final destination.

Contingent Cargo Policies—This type of insurance policy is for an event where a third party who is directly responsible for the cargo does not have the insurance or maybe is underinsured for the damage or loss of value to the cargo while it is in their custody and control. Therefore this type of coverage is a secondary insurance policy to the primary insurance policy in the event the primary insurance does not cover or is not in place to cover the loss. A contingent policy may also apply when a carrier causes damage or just may refuse to deliver the cargo or for some reason refuses to accept liability for a loss or damage to the goods during the time it was in their control.

Shipper's Interest—This type of insurance policy is for coverage needed when the value of the load is greater than the amount of insurance being carried by the carrier that is slated to haul the shipment.

The key is to retain an experienced cargo insurance agent who understands the different cargo insurance products and can review the transportation/cargo contracts to determine the amount and type of cargo insurance needed. Coverage has to be secured in advance of the trip and exclusions should be identified to eliminate "gaps in coverage" that may expose a carrier to a large uninsured exposure.

With the advent of the fictitious pick-up scam currently, insurance coverage is being tested in new ways. Recently after a fictitious or fraudulent pick-up, the shipper filed a claim against a carrier that did not make the pick-up as they were a victim of the identity theft. The shipper stated that the carrier was still responsible for the loss since they had the duty to protect their identity and not allow it to be stolen. This is all facts for lawyers and courts to work out but it does go back to protecting your own company and having awareness to current cargo criminal methods. I am sure the shipper's broker made several errors that would make it very difficult to push liability over to the identity theft victimized carrier.

Conclusion

I have given a technology/solution for in-transit security, warehouses and facilities. There are many others I could offer but these are my number one recommendations in those areas. I also have been working on a solution for identity theft and fictitious pick-up gangs. My system will vet a carrier to eliminate the identity theft angles involved with this crime. Further, the program will vet a carrier to a brokerage company's guidelines and then provide compliance and audit processes to maintain the vetting status to the requirements.

The current problem is age old: companies are reluctant to change the ways they operate. As long as they continue down their current path, they will continue to be victimized. They must slow the carrier selection process and initiate real checks and balances to avoid being targeted for fraud. They do not have to do it for every carrier, but they must do it for any carrier they plan to use for high value or the known high risk commodity loads discussed in this book. The vetting must include a close inspection of all of the required DOT documents, insurance coverage and exclusions, a site inspection, and references.

Recently, the SC-ISAC had eight loads reported stolen by fictitious pick-up. This crime is increasing daily and will not stop until companies take the correct steps. I collaborated with a company called C-Net Technologies and we put together two programs for transportation. One was a carrier management system for brokerage to vet carriers for their high value clients as mentioned above. The other is a transportation specific background screening program for hiring drivers. Both programs were designed as solutions for known problems in the industry. The SWTSC isn't a social alliance; it provides law enforcement training and the BOLO/Alert program and strives to find solutions for problems, resources, and providers which can assist our membership and the industry. I keep information on all types of different services and products relative to our transportation scope of work, and I continually make referrals to industry members. There are many service providers and products that I can recommend based on their service and effectiveness.

The key to security in all areas is using a multi-layered approach in all phases. Whether it is facility, in-transit, personnel, or procedural security, it is best handled if done in common sense and logical layers to provide the best protection and results. The goal is prevention in a cost efficient manner. When you scroll through the SWTSC Best Practices above, all may not be relevant to your operation but they will act as a good reminder for process, procedure, and products that can be used to best secure your company's operation.

As far as insurance coverage for cargo goes, the same *Insurance Journal* Internet edition contained an article about CargoNet and its position as the insurance industry tie-in to the cargo theft information sharing and networking. We have discussed that point several times throughout this book but, as it said in that article, the public/private partnership involving the transportation industry, law enforcement, and the insurance industry is definitely building.

Chapter 7

Moving Forward

Introduction

I would hope from all the information which has been presented thus far, it is apparent to the industry and its members that we must do all we can to protect ourselves. It is incumbent upon the industry and its members to take the necessary steps to protect one's own operation. By taking the security steps necessary to protect one's company and operation from theft, we are also preventing interference and disturbance from other possible harm including terrorist acts. Taking the initiative to take the necessary steps to protecting our own companies will make our operations more efficient and less susceptive to business continuity issues and disruptions.

Essential Decisions for Industry

During the writing of this book, which occurred between January and April 2012, several things happened relative to cargo theft which affected the industry and law enforcement.

We will talk about several of those things, but first we need to stress the need of involvement in the industry councils, law enforcement networking, and pushing for the needs of the industry through initiatives such as the National Cargo Theft Task Force. These are not initiatives which take countless time or money, just participation and effort.

One of the most important go-forward actions should be to further enhance the information sharing and networking. This is currently in process with the addition of a new industry council for Virginia and the Carolinas. The way they are being set-up will provide another partner in the BOLO/Alert program which will not only strengthen what is currently in place but also give a broader reach for the current communication network. Also with the evolution of CargoNet being sponsored by the insurance industry, the network and communication system can be greatly expanded through its ISO and law enforcement connections. Driving more cargo theft data into the collection databases will allow for further analysis and more information and awareness concerning cargo crime issues. More communication, more data, more information sharing, and more law enforcement networking will overcome the lack of a government enforcement response.

Every new change or implementation that has come in the transportation security arena that I have seen has come in low, slow doses. It has been baby steps to get us where we are today, although much has been accomplished. We can get it done through the current sources and resources by just continuing to push forward. This will not take a bunch of money, just the effort to get the problem recognized by the right parties. As an industry, transportation pays a ton of taxes and the supply chain industries deserve our share of service from the law enforcement agencies paid with our tax dollars. We can't sit quietly in the corner and allow district attorneys to decide not to take a case because it is a driver give-up. The law does not allow district attorneys to pick and choose which types of theft they will prosecute. We can't sit back and let the government make all kinds of regulations, but provide no resources for cargo theft. This is not a one-way street, although lately it seems that way. Through awareness and bringing attention to the problems and issues, more can be done. Letting the right people know and getting the right people involved will assist in getting the attention needed.

One major need to be pursued is the establishment of a cargo theft statute in each state of the union to pair with the Federal Cargo Theft UCR statute. This statute needs to provide enhanced penalties for cargo theft and organized cargo theft along with language making the theft of a (police operation) sting trailer a felony offense not based on the value of the stolen goods.

Below is a rough draft of a soon to be proposed Cargo Theft Statute which is being prepared for introduction to the legislature in Texas. This is being drawn up NICB Agent Stacy Hohenberger, with input from several parties, and it is not yet completed. Having this statute in the Texas Penal Code will make prosecution easier and more specific to a cargo crime. Language still needs to be added concerning the sting trailers. This will also give the state a better statute to pursue prosecuting the driver give-up situation and other related cargo crime.

Sec. 31.17. CARGO THEFT AND ORGANIZED CARGO THEFT:

(a) "Cargo theft" is defined as the criminal taking any commercial shipment of cargo moving via a pipeline system, trucks, railroad cars, ships, aircraft, an intermodal container, intermodal chassis, trailer, or other vehicle from point of origin to final destination, regardless of any temporary stop while awaiting transshipment or otherwise, including any tank or storage facility, station house, platform, depot, wharf, air terminal, airport, aircraft terminal, air navigation facility, container freight station, warehouse, freight distribution facility, or freight consolidation facility.

US H.R. 3199 (USA Patriot Act Improvement and Re-authorization Act of 2005)

(b) In this section "cargo" is considered but not limited to the following:

(1) articles,

(2) articles of commerce,

(3) assets,

(4) belongings,

(5) capital goods,

(6) cargo,

(7) chattel,

(8) consumer durables,

(9) consumer goods,

(10) contents,

(11) effects,

(12) freight,

(13) goods,

(14) goods for sale,

(15) items for sale,

(16) line,

(17) line of goods,

(18) manufactured goods,

(19) material assets,

(20) materials,

(21) merchandise,

(22) movables,

(23) possessions,

(24) produce,

(25) property,

(26) res venales,

(27) salable commodities,

(28) shop goods,

(29) staples,

(30) stock,

(31) stock in trade,

(32) store,

(33) supplies,

(34) tangible assets,

(35) vendibles and

(36) wares

(c) A person commits an offense if the person intentionally or knowingly conducts, promotes, or facilitates an activity in which the person receives, possesses, conceals, stores, barters, sells, or disposes of a total value of not less than $1,500 of:

(1) stolen cargo; or

(2) cargo explicitly represented to the person as being stolen cargo.

(d) An offense under this section is:

(1) a state jail felony if the total value of the merchandise involved in the activity is $1,500 or more but less than $20,000;

(2) a felony of the third degree if the total value of the merchandise involved in the activity is $20,000 or more but less than $100,000;

(3) a felony of the second degree if the total value of the merchandise involved in the activity is $100,000 or more but less than $200,000; or

(4) A felony of the first degree if the total value of the merchandise involved in the activity is $200,000 or more.

(e) An offense described for purposes of punishment by Subsections (d)(1)-(3) is increased to the next higher category of offense if it is shown on the trial of the offense that the person organized, supervised, financed, or managed one or more other persons engaged in an activity described by Subsection (d).

(f) For the purposes of punishment, an offense under this section is increased to the next highest category of offense if the cargo taken was a controlled substance as defined by the Texas Health and Safety Code, Section 481.001 (1)(5) or controlled substance analogue as defined by the Texas Health and Safety Code, Section 481.001 (1)(6).

(g) It is not a defense to prosecution under this section that:

(1) the offense occurred as a result of a deception or strategy on the part of a law enforcement agency, including the use of an undercover operative or peace officer;

(2) the actor was provided by a law enforcement agency with a facility in which to commit the offense or an opportunity to engage in conduct constituting the offense; or

(3) the actor was solicited to commit the offense by a peace officer, and the solicitation was of a type that would encourage a person predisposed to commit the offense to actually commit the offense, but would not encourage a person not predisposed to commit the offense to actually commit the offense.

Source: Hohenberger 2012.

The above is a good first step for getting this in the Texas Penal Code and closing existing loop holes for cargo thieves. This effort needs to be taken up by every state in the United States where one does not exist. Why is it needed? Very simple.

I looked in the index of the Texas Penal Code and the word Cargo is not even listed. No reference to that word appears anywhere in the code. Read the current penal code for theft, from the 2010 Texas Penal Code below. Nothing is mentioned about cargo in this statute and thus leaves much to be desired when enforcing the law related to cargo theft and the district attorneys in some jurisdictions not wanting to prosecute driver involved type offenses.

CHAPTER 31. THEFT

§ 31.03. THEFT.

(a) A person commits an offense if he unlawfully appropriates property with intent to deprive the owner of property.

(b) Appropriation of property is unlawful if:

   (1) it is without the owner's effective consent;

   (2) the property is stolen and the actor appropriates the property knowing it was stolen by another; or

   (3) property in the custody of any law enforcement agency was explicitly represented by any law enforcement agent to the actor as being stolen and the actor appropriates the property believing it was stolen by another.

(c) For purposes of Subsection (b):

   (1) evidence that the actor has previously participated in recent transactions other than, but similar to, that which the prosecution is based is admissible for the purpose of showing knowledge or intent and the issues of knowledge or intent are raised by the actor's plea of not guilty;

   (2) the testimony of an accomplice shall be corroborated by proof that tends to connect the

actor to the crime, but the actor's knowledge or intent may be established by the uncorroborated testimony of the accomplice;

(3) an actor engaged in the business of buying and selling used or secondhand personal property, or lending money on the security of personal property deposited with the actor, is presumed to know upon receipt by the actor of stolen property (other than a motor vehicle subject to Chapter 501, Transportation Code) that the property has been previously stolen from another if the actor pays for or loans against the property $25 or more (or consideration of equivalent value) and the actor knowingly or recklessly:

(A) fails to record the name, address, and physical description or identification number of the seller or pledgor;

(B) fails to record a complete description of the property, including the serial number, if reasonably available, or other identifying characteristics; or

(C) fails to obtain a signed warranty from the seller or pledgor that the seller or pledgor has the right to possess the property. It is the express intent of this provision that the presumption arises unless the actor complies with each of the numbered requirements;

(4) for the purposes of Subdivision (3)(A), "identification number" means driver's license number, military identification number, identification certificate, or other official number capable of identifying an individual;

(5) stolen property does not lose its character as stolen when recovered by any law enforcement agency;

(6) an actor engaged in the business of obtaining abandoned or wrecked motor vehicles or parts of an abandoned or wrecked motor vehicle for resale, disposal, scrap, repair, rebuilding, demolition, or other form of salvage is presumed to know on receipt by the actor of stolen property that the property has been previously stolen from another if the actor knowingly or recklessly:

(A) fails to maintain an accurate and legible inventory of each motor vehicle component part purchased by or delivered to the actor, including the date of purchase or delivery, the name, age, address, sex, and driver's license number of the seller or person making the delivery, the license plate number of the motor vehicle in which the part was delivered, a complete description of the part, and the vehicle identification number of the motor vehicle from which the part was removed, or in lieu of maintaining an inventory, fails to record the name and certificate of inventory number of the person who dismantled the motor vehicle from which the part was obtained;

(B) fails on receipt of a motor vehicle to obtain a certificate of authority, sales receipt, or transfer document as required by Chapter 683, Transportation Code, or a certificate of title showing that the motor vehicle is not subject to a lien or that all recorded liens on the motor vehicle have been released; or

(C) fails on receipt of a motor vehicle to immediately remove an unexpired license plate from the motor vehicle, to keep the plate in a secure and locked place, or to maintain an inventory, on forms provided by the Texas Department of Transportation, of license plates kept under this paragraph, including for each plate or set of plates the license plate number and the make, motor number, and vehicle identification number of the motor vehicle from which the plate was removed;

(7) an actor who purchases or receives a used or secondhand motor vehicle is presumed to know on receipt by the actor of the motor vehicle that the motor vehicle has been previously stolen from another if the actor knowingly or recklessly:

(A) fails to report to the Texas Department of Transportation the failure of the person who sold or delivered the motor vehicle to the actor to deliver to the actor a properly executed certificate of title to the motor vehicle at the time the motor vehicle was delivered; or

(B) fails to file with the county tax assessor-collector of the county in which the actor received the motor vehicle, not later than the 20th day after the date the actor received the motor vehicle, the registration license receipt and certificate of title or evidence of title delivered to the actor in accordance with Subchapter D, Chapter 520, Transportation Code, at the time the motor vehicle was delivered;

(8) an actor who purchases or receives from any source other than a licensed retailer or distributor of pesticides a restricted-use pesticide or a state-limited-use pesticide or

a compound, mixture, or preparation containing a restricted-use or state-limited-use pesticide is presumed to know on receipt by the actor of the pesticide or compound, mixture, or preparation that the pesticide or compound, mixture, or preparation has been previously stolen from another if the actor:
   (A) fails to record the name, address, and physical description of the seller or pledgor;
   (B) fails to record a complete description of the amount and type of pesticide or compound, mixture, or preparation purchased or received; and
   (C) fails to obtain a signed warranty from the seller or pledgor that the seller or pledgor has the right to possess the property; and
(9) an actor who is subject to Section 409, Packers and Stockyards Act (7 U.S.C. Section 228b), that obtains livestock from a commission merchant by representing that the actor will make prompt payment is presumed to have induced the commission merchant's consent by deception if the actor fails to make full payment in accordance with Section 409, Packers and Stockyards Act (7 U.S.C. Section 228b).

(d) It is not a defense to prosecution under this section that:
   (1) the offense occurred as a result of a deception or strategy on the part of a law enforcement agency, including the use of an undercover operative or peace officer;
   (2) the actor was provided by a law enforcement agency with a facility in which to commit the offense or an opportunity to engage in conduct constituting the offense; or

(3) the actor was solicited to commit the offense by a peace officer, and the solicitation was of a type that would encourage a person predisposed to commit the offense to actually commit the offense, but would not encourage a person not predisposed to commit the offense to actually commit the offense.

(e) Except as provided by Subsection (f), an offense under this section is:

(1) a Class C misdemeanor if the value of the property stolen is less than:

(A) $50; or

(B) $20 and the defendant obtained the property by issuing or passing a check or similar sight order in a manner described by Section 31.06;

(2) a Class B misdemeanor if:

(A) the value of the property stolen is:

(i) $50 or more but less than $500; or

(ii) $20 or more but less than $500 and the defendant obtained the property by issuing or passing a check or similar sight order in a manner described by Section 31.06; or

(B) the value of the property stolen is less than:

(i) $50 and the defendant has previously been convicted of any grade of theft; or

(ii) $20, the defendant has previously been convicted of any grade of theft, and the defendant obtained the property by issuing or passing a check or similar sight order in a manner described by Section 31.06;

(3) a Class A misdemeanor if the value of the property stolen is $500 or more but less than $1,500;

(4) a state jail felony if:
   (A) the value of the property stolen is $1,500 or more but less than $20,000, or the property is less than 10 head of cattle, horses, or exotic livestock or exotic fowl as defined by Section 142.001, Agriculture Code, or any part thereof under the value of $20,000, or less than 100 head of sheep, swine, or goats or any part thereof under the value of $20,000;
   (B) regardless of value, the property is stolen from the person of another or from a human corpse or grave;
   (C) the property stolen is a firearm, as defined by Section46.01;
   (D) the value of the property stolen is less than $1,500 and the defendant has been previously convicted two or more times of any grade of theft; or
   (E) the property stolen is an official ballot or official carrier envelope for an election;
(5) a felony of the third degree if the value of the property stolen is $20,000 or more but less than $100,000, or the property is:
   (A) 10 or more head of cattle, horses, or exotic livestock or exotic fowl as defined by Section 142.001, Agriculture Code, stolen during a single transaction and having an aggregate value of less than $100,000; or
   (B) 100 or more head of sheep, swine, or goats stolen during a single transaction and having an aggregate value of less than $100,000;
(6) a felony of the second degree if the value of the property stolen is $100,000 or more but less than $200,000; or

(7) a felony of the first degree if the value of the property stolen is $200,000 or more.

(f) An offense described for purposes of punishment by Subsections (e)(1)-(6) is increased to the next higher category of offense if it is shown on the trial of the offense that:

(1) the actor was a public servant at the time of the offense and the property appropriated came into the actor's custody, possession, or control by virtue of his status as a public servant;

(2) the actor was in a contractual relationship with government at the time of the offense and the property appropriated came into the actor's custody, possession, or control by virtue of the contractual relationship; or

(3) the owner of the property appropriated was at the time of the offense an elderly individual.

(g) For the purposes of Subsection (a), a person is the owner of exotic livestock or exotic fowl as defined by Section 142.001, Agriculture Code, only if the person qualifies to claim the animal under Section 142.0021, Agriculture Code, if the animal is an stray.

(h) In this section:

(1) "Restricted-use pesticide" means a pesticide classified as a restricted-use pesticide by the administrator of the Environmental Protection Agency under 7 U.S.C. Section 136a, as that law existed on January 1, 1995, and containing an active ingredient listed in the federal regulations adopted under that law (40 C.F.R. Section 152.175) and in effect on that date.

(2) "State-limited-use pesticide" means a pesticide classified as a state-limited-use pesticide

by the Department of Agriculture under Section 76.003, Agriculture Code, as that section existed on January 1, 1995, and containing an active ingredient listed in the rules adopted under that section (4 TAC Section 7.24) as that section existed on that date.

(i) For purposes of Subsection (c) (9), "livestock" and "commission merchant" have the meanings assigned by Section 147.001, Agriculture Code.

(j) With the consent of the appropriate local county or district attorney, the attorney general has concurrent jurisdiction with that consenting local prosecutor to prosecute an offense under this section that involves the state Medicaid program.

Source: Texas 2010.

This is the current Texas law and it makes no reference to Cargo in the entire statute. That does not prevent this statute from being used to prosecute cargo thieves but is not nearly as specific as the proposed statute. This law currently does not match up well with the Cargo Theft UCR shown in Chapter 1 and makes it difficult to match up the UCR reporting in Texas to the Federal Code. Obtaining a specific cargo theft statute is very important to being able to place a bit more significance in the law and make it more easily enforceable. After reading both entries, you can make your own determination.

In the states which have been identified in Chapter 1, an effort should be made to either organize a multi-agency cargo theft task force or to strengthen the existing ones.

Why are task forces so important? As a former police officer who has worked numerous investigations, the simple fact is that when an investigative group is allowed to specialize or focus on certain types of crime, the group becomes much more involved in the overall intelligence aspect of that criminal activity, thus enhancing their investigative abilities.

They also have time to focus on the persons arrested for the offenses, interview them while they are in custody, and build an investigative "hook book" of suspects, fences, and associates. This collected intelligence leads to further information about involved parties and accomplices along with information about where the stolen property is being sold or delivered, which, in turn, leads to the development of informants and all types of related investigative information.

Once this investigative process is in place, the Task Force Officers (TFOs) have many more options when a theft occurs than just working the case without the background and information that true investigative techniques bring forth. It is really no different than a long-term narcotics or organized crime investigation with the goal of identifying the players and locating the big fish or the buyers so that those persons can be charged and put out of business. This will not happen if you do not have a focused investigative effort. Blind luck is good for investigators but working hard, building information and intelligence will get you much further when dealing with organized criminal groups. That is why we need cargo theft task forces in several major areas so that those types of investigative inroads can be created. These task forces could also start networking and communicating and sharing information which would lead to tying together other associates and related crimes and criminal activities.

Remember earlier when we discussed high value warehouse burglaries, the DNA of one of the suspects of several warehouse burglaries around the country has been matched to DNA found in a pharmaceutical burglary in Enfield, Connecticut. These were not local criminal acts; these involve the organized, traveling, professional criminal elements. Single, one-time investigations will seldom connect the dots, matching information from these types of activities which occur in very distant and distinct jurisdictions.

Lobbying for Cargo Theft Task Forces and Cargo Crime Programs

Through the National Cargo Theft Task Force, a lobbying and legislative effort has been started. This part of the NCTTF program needs to be enhanced and cargo crime awareness brought to the attention of both federal and state legislators. The goal would be to get cargo theft statutes passed in all of the states and to bring the need for a better cargo theft and cargo related crime response to the attention of federal law enforcement agencies.

The crimes themselves are starting to get attention from federal agencies. Just recently, on March 23, 2012, the Food and Drug Administration released an agency program directive titled "FDA's Response to Cargo Thefts." The purpose of the document was to establish a general procedure by which the agency would respond to a cargo theft involving an FDA-regulated product. The directive spoke to established procedures for product removal from the market, public notice, and handling medical product shortages. The purpose of the directive was to also ensure that the FDA's regulatory response to cargo thefts is consistent and effective.

The SOP addresses FDA's response to cargo thefts of FDA-regulated products as determined by the Office of Regulatory Affairs (ORA), Office of Criminal Investigations (OCI), and the Commissioner's Office via the Cargo Theft Response Team (CTRT), a workgroup comprised of representatives from those parts of FDA. The Office of Criminal Investigations will lead the criminal investigation for the agency and will communicate/coordinate with other federal, state, and local law enforcement agencies. The Office of Enforcement will coordinate the Agency's regulatory response to the potential public health concerns associated with the stolen products re-entering the market, coordinate the development of the appropriate regulatory response to the firm's action plan regarding the theft through the CTRT, and will ensure dissemination of public notification of cargo theft incidences whether issued by FDA or the firm(s).

OCI's primary objective related to cargo theft investigations is to identify, target, and dismantle illicit prescription drug diversion networks that threaten the legitimate pharmaceutical supply chain. FDA considers cargo thefts to include tractor-trailer and warehouse thefts of FDA-regulated products, including prescription drugs, OTC drug products, infant formula, and medical devices which may pose a threat to the public health or a risk to the legitimate supply chain. OCI cargo theft investigations may be initiated because the criminal organizations behind such thefts are suspected of being associated with drug diversion networks. (Administration 2012)

You can see the full directive by going to Staff Manual Guides, Volume IV. The fact is that several things that happened here are good for the industry. A federal agency has taken note that there is a problem with cargo thefts and it has established a way to respond. In its directive, the agency also makes reference to the Pharmaceutical Cargo Security Coalition (PCSC) and proclaims to be a member of that group. The agency also recognizes this group's mission is to share information and identify emerging trends while working together to better secure pharmaceutical products in-transit. This is probably the first federal agency to mention an industry council and actually give it credit and authentication. Even though the directive appears more regulatory toward the firms involved rather than toward the cargo criminals, it is still good to open up other possible federal jurisdictions for prosecution. Now if we can get several other federal agencies to understand there is an issue and obtain federal investigation and jurisdictional assistance, we will have taken a significant step toward eliminating the criminal enterprises involved in this illicit activity. We have to hope it will not string a bunch of regulations into place without offering any true assistance with the cause of the problem.

Cargo theft is not the only cargo crime which needs a more focused federal response in relation to drugs and contraband interdiction. Once again, when contraband enters a commercial vehicle conveyance and/or transportation lane, it seldom begins and ends in the same local or even same state jurisdiction. As we discussed earlier, there are real and known profiles and intelligence from these types of shipments that could be used to spotlight the illicit shippers.

While I was still working for the transportation company, Detective Ed Matis from the Dallas–Fort Worth Interdiction Task Force took an interest in our industry and began attending council meetings and working freight interdiction as part of his duty with the DFW Drug Interdiction Task Force. As he met more and more of the company security managers, he started coming to the docks and bringing a dog handler to scan the freight on the dock. After a time, he realized that this was an exercise in futility. We began talking to him about the known profiles that could be associated with just about every contraband shipment, and he began to understand how those factors could be used to put together a comprehensive commercial vehicle interdiction program. Eventually, Ed put together an investigative proposal for his DFW Task Force which he called "Bordernet." This proposal, which was never accepted or acted upon, put together several key features to partner with the industry to identify suspicious shipments placed into the commercial commerce lanes and to protect carrier company personnel on the border from the threats of the cartel.

When I was in the industry, terminal managers on the border had fears about reporting suspicious shipments and having law enforcement respond to their locations. We had a manager at one border location threatened, and he did not want to deal with the issue locally. Many times when reported at the origin terminal, the local police would respond and take possession of the shipment leading to no follow-up or controlled delivery being completed. It is much worse on the border now. It makes much more sense now to investigate a package identified as suspicious, at the first break point, thus removing the local anxiety and border difficulty. This also allows for law enforcement at the break bulk to be notified as to exact time of the suspicious shipment's arrival so that law enforcement can be present to meet the shipment at the time when it arrives for consolidation at the Freight Assembly Center.

By getting a pre-alert concerning its arrival, the TFOs have time to research the shipper, shipment, and consignee. They can have the paperwork ready for a search warrant and have a canine and dog handler present to immediately scan the shipment. If it is contraband, the TFOs would be able to make a determination as to how it would be handled from that point on. If it is not contraband, it could be quickly released and moved on through the consolidation process. This makes a lot of sense. See significant parts of the proposal below. I believe this type of program would reap huge benefits for both the industry and law enforcement. This type of enforcement program would act to enhance finding shipments involving contrabands other than narcotics as well.

Bordernet

We are proposing the development of a network of terminal managers (TM)/freight employees in LTL freight companies in Laredo and McAllen/Brownsville, and other border areas that can identify shipments with suspicious characteristics. The initial profile that we would use would make this easy for the freight companies and would consist of characteristics that have been the most common on previous seizures and are the easiest to track. The characteristics we would like to target are: 1) Dock drop off at the border terminal, and 2) cash, money order or pre-paid credit card payments by shippers or other suspicious activity observed at the terminal or in the paperwork. The shipment at this time would be considered suspicious, but would not necessarily contain contraband. The TFOs have learned from speaking with terminal managers along the border with hubs in Dallas/Houston that approximately ten to fifty shipments per week meet this criteria coming through Dallas and Houston. With the ability to inspect this volume of freight which has suspicious characteristics, the seizure success rate would greatly increase.

Upon the border terminals identifying suspicious shipments, a protocol developed between the freight companies and freight interdiction units to report the suspicious shipments would be established in Dallas/Houston. By contacting freight interdiction units in Dallas/Houston, this would solve the problems which TFOs have been told are reasons the freight industry did not care to report suspicious freight. The first reason, financial, would be solved because the freight would not be waiting on the border dock. When the suspicious freight was observed, the freight would be loaded as normal and depart the border terminal. The time of arrival/departure/delivery, PRO#, bill of lading, and other billing information would be forwarded to freight interdiction units in Dallas/Houston to be researched.

By the freight interdiction units receiving this information in Dallas/Houston five to nine hours before the freight reaches those terminals, TFOs would be able to research the information establishing any connections to other cases, set up technical support for the surveillance, and prepare a search warrant if information warrants. Due to the fact that narcotic traffickers shipping through freight companies often track their shipments through the freight company web pages, this advanced notice will help by being "invisible" to narcotic traffickers. By working within the parameters set by the freight companies and moving the freight, the traffickers will not be alerted to law enforcements involvement. If the suspicious shipment is unable to be cleared in a timely fashion, the freight would continue moving within the system and be checked by LEOs at the next transfer point. When the shipment arrived at the hub/destination terminal, the freight interdiction contact using narcotic detecting canine and other research tools would either establish probable cause for a warrant or clear the shipment.

The second reason, safety, would be solved by the freight following normal shipping protocol and the fact that only a limited number of freight employees would be aware the freight was being tracked. Law enforcement officers (LEO) liaisons at the border would be contacted by freight interdiction units in Dallas/Houston regarding positive, suspicious shipments freeing those officers/agents from the responsibility of having to check out this large volume of freight.

By LEOs not having a physical presence at the freight docks it is less likely that the other freight employees would notify traffickers of their freight being identified as suspicious. The freight identified as suspicious in this program would normally not come to the attention of LEOs at the border. Officers/agents working at the border will continue to get tips on freight, which in the past has been identified by traditional means. By developing relationships with freight terminals at the border, these investigations should also be enhanced because of the resulting better cooperation and understanding. We feel that implementing the above program will improve the amount of intelligence regarding suspicious freight shipments received and reduce the volume of freight to be reviewed making it manageable. The intelligence received not only will be expanded to the destination cities but back to the border cities in which the shipment originated.

As a result of the events of 9/11, the freight industry is under scrutiny by the government to control criminal activity and potential terrorist activities. The freight industry would benefit by being given a way to report suspicious shipments and alleviate their fears of threats and loss of revenue by policing themselves. It has been found that drug organizations are embedded into the freight industry and have been using freight to move their drug shipments throughout the country. By making the freight industry employees more comfortable in reporting this activity, we can draw on their expertise to identify and uncover these shipments and organizations.

The "net" part of Bordernet would consist of freight interdiction units off the border in Dallas/Fort Worth, Houston, and El Paso working to set up a network of officers/agents willing to receive information and work together to develop the information to the fullest with LEO liaisons on the border in Laredo and McAllen/Brownsville. Officers/agents would use their contacts within the LTL freight industry to develop SOIs to track suspicious freight. Members of the DFWTF have contacted officers/agents in Houston and El Paso regarding working freight interdiction. Officers/agents in Laredo, McAllen, and other border cities who have been found to work with freight companies have been contacted to liaison on the border. All of the above locations have shown interest in coordinating intelligence received from border freight terminals and conducting investigations.

Since 9/11, the New York City Police Intelligence Unit has taken a different approach to identifying terrorist looking at New York City as a target. The NYPD has developed the "NEXUS" program which is basically developing relationships with legitimate businesses to report suspicious activity, "interdiction." The NYPD has also assigned detectives to foreign countries to liaison with intelligence units to see what is coming at New York from places where terrorism originates. Bordernet is similar in concept attempting to look at the drug and contraband problem from a different angle and knowing what we are dealing with before it arrives in Dallas/Fort Worth or Houston. We are not taking away from the efforts of officers/agents at the border, but enhancing the capability to identify narcotic trafficking organizations which would fly under the radar.

We have been told by the freight industry that these characteristics have been observed in the past. When contacted, we have been successful on many occasions in making seizures and uncovering organizations. This program is not trying to move in on the other's territory, but rather to enhance and utilize an untapped resource. A hundred percent of zero still equals zero. If we cannot get this industry to work with us, and if we cannot work with each other, we are missing a great resource!

Procedures and Resources to Develop Bordernet

The Freight Industry

- Work with contacts/SOI's developed by freight interdiction units in Dallas/Fort Worth, Houston, and El Paso to develop to identify potential contacts/SOI's in McAllen/Brownsville, Laredo, El Paso, and other border areas.
- Travel to Laredo and McAllen/Brownsville area terminals to discreetly meet with terminal managers and conduct training to set up the program and develop their trust. Border LEO liaisons would be introduced as border liaisons/contacts during these meetings.
- Develop protocols working with representatives of the freight industry to establish how information regarding suspicious shipments is relayed to law enforcement (through security directors versus directly from TMs to "net" LEOs. Phone versus e-mail or terminal access).
- Set initial criteria of characteristics for suspicious shipments to be:
  1. "Dock drop off" at the border terminals.
  2. Cash or money order or pre-paid credit card payment by shipper or other suspicious activity observed at the terminal or in the paperwork. The shipment at this time would be considered "suspicious" and would be sent as a normal shipment.

All shipments with the above characteristics would be considered suspicious shipments at the border terminals and would not be treated any differently than a normal shipment. The shipment would depart the terminal to Dallas, Houston, or other hub along with other freight. The SOI at the terminal would follow the contact protocol and notify "net" LEOs of the suspicious shipment prior to departure of the trailer. (Contact prior to departure is necessary due to the Border Patrol conducting checkpoints off the border and possibly intercepting the suspicious shipment. By prior knowledge by "net" LEOs the release of the driver/tractor trailer may be expedited).

- The information needed regarding the suspicious shipment would be: PRO #, time of arrival at hub/destination terminal, time of departure or delivery from hub/destination terminal, bill of lading/manifest information (shipper/consignee: names, addresses, phone numbers, weight, listed contents, quote price, price paid, form of payment), suspect description, vehicle description and identification shown upon shipping.
- Freight companies should always receive full payment upon shipping, or as soon as suspects arrive to pick up freight on "dock pickups." If the shipment is reweighed upon arrival at destination terminal and discrepancy is found, the suspect should be advised he will have to pay for the discrepancy before receiving the shipment (benefits LEOs/freight company by having suspect possibly leave and identify co-conspirators/get freight company money due).

Bordernet Law Enforcement

- Develop and meet with law enforcement liaison contacts in McAllen/Brownsville, Laredo, El Paso, and other border areas that may currently have contacts within the freight industry interested in coordinating intelligence information and conducting investigations within the network where it will do the most good developing cases and intelligence to the fullest.

■ Establish contact list and meet with officers/agents working the "net" in Dallas/Fort Worth, Houston, and El Paso checking the availability resources (narcotic detecting canine, officers, travel funds, etc.) and commitment to the program to be able to efficiently work the suspicious freight within the parameters set by normal shipments.

■ Prior to the suspicious shipment arriving at the hub/destination terminal the information being received from the SOI approximately five to nine hours before by "net" LEOs/analysts in Dallas/Houston should be researched for any criminal history or related cases. The addresses should be verified to see what is at that location and search warrant can be prepared documenting observed characteristics and researched information.

■ Upon the suspicious shipment arriving at the hub/destination terminal the shipment will be met by "net" LEOs and a narcotic detecting canine. The suspicious shipment should be removed from the trailer and placed on the dock in an area not to disturb the normal flow of the dock. The suspicious shipment should be checked by a narcotic detecting canine for the presence of a narcotic odor and reweighed for any weight discrepancy. A description, measurements, and photographs of all sides of the shipment should be taken. Upon probable cause being developed a search warrant should be received as soon as possible to stay within the parameters set for the departure/delivery time. (Search warrants are recommended due to the evidence possibly being inadmissible in court by administratively opening shipment under freight company's authority to inspect freight/freight companies potentially become agents of the government by the training received and advising to look for suspicious freight.)

■ If the suspicious shipment is found to be negative for canine alert and no probable cause developed, the shipment will be considered clear and will remain in the care of the freight company to continue in the freight system. If the shipment is a transfer shipment and cannot be checked or cleared between the time of arrival and departure, LEOs at the next transfer point would be contacted to check the suspicious shipment.

■ Upon a search warrant being received for the suspicious shipment, the shipment will be carefully opened and inspected to preserve the package for a possible controlled delivery. If contraband is found in the shipment, the evidence will be photographed, fingerprinted, and documented. If a controlled delivery is to be attempted, the evidence will remain or be removed pending the advice of the AUSA/DA. Technical equipment (tracking device/package beacon) should be installed upon establishing surveillance for a controlled delivery. If the shipment is a transfer shipment going to other parts of the country, contact should be made with LEOs at the destination city. If destination LEOs are interested in conducting a controlled delivery, the evidence should be removed and the package should be reconstructed as accurately as possible. The shipment should then continue within the freight system. (Check with freight company to make sure "no" notations have been made within the freight company tracking system. Narcotic traffickers track shipments for any deviation on freight company websites.) Arrangements should be made to transport the contraband to the destination city for a controlled delivery.

■ Upon no interest by destination city to conduct a controlled delivery, remove and process the evidence. The package should be reconstructed as accurately as possible and should continue within the freight system to the destination city. Local law enforcement could be contacted at the destination city to conduct a traffic stop and identify suspect upon shipment being delivered by a freight company. Intelligence received can be documented and distributed to the originating and destination cities.

Future: Bordernet Computer Scanning

The Bordernet program is an evolution of traditional interdiction; the next stage in the evolution of interdiction regarding freight interdiction would be "computer scanning." This program is similar to the hijacker profile that the FAA used to track characteristics which identified potential hijackers. This program would give us the ability to review even more freight and eliminate the time constraints put on employees reviewing manually. Even though we would always have the need to learn from the "expertise" of freight employees, this would give us the ability to check freight which has met the characteristics set. In some cases, employees might see shipments with characteristics that they are too busy to check or notify us.

In working with the freight industry in the past, we have found that there is the ability to tap into the LTL freight companies' computerized billing information and identify characteristics which have been found to be common on a number of freight seizures which were observed to be suspicious. We know of at least one freight company security director who was able to develop a computer program with his IT unit that would scan shipments for characteristics and identify suspicious freight containing narcotics, currency, and other illegal items. This security director stated, "My IT guys had this installed in less than two hours." We have found by talking with representatives of the freight industry that the ASA 400 is the most common base operating system currently used in the freight industry to track billing information. Representatives who have systems other than the ASA 400 have said that this program can be adapted to other systems also.

The program we would like to develop would be working with corporate/security in the freight companies where the

computer would watch certain cities known for narcotic trafficking, possible terrorist activity, or other illegal activity. The
computer would be programmed to scan for some of the following characteristics: shipping routes, form of payment, how
delivered/received, weight discrepancies, coded to un-coded,
addresses, person to person, business names, phone numbers,
or cost-to-profit ratio. If the computer observes a shipment
containing at least two of the identified characteristics, the
PRO # is then emailed to a company security investigator. The
bill is then reviewed further to see if it is a common customer
or should be investigated further. If the shipment is found to
be suspicious, it would be referred to a freight interdiction unit
to be investigated as suspicious freight.

Since 9/11, we have all heard that we need to tighten up
security with regard to terrorism. We have also heard that
the Department of Homeland Security would like to implement
rules on the freight companies to tighten security in the freight
industry. We hope that if we can implement this program we can
give the freight industry a proactive approach to scanning for
narcotics, contraband, illegal weapons, people, and other terrorist related activity. We feel that it would be much better for the
freight industry to show it is policing its own business and doing
everything possible to identify and keep illegal shipments out of
the freight industry, than be told how policing should be done.

The advantage to law enforcement would be that a greater
amount of freight would be reviewed with characteristics
which have been found on prior seizures. This would increase
the probability that more seizures would be made. The characteristics could be periodically adjusted in the computer to
reflect changing trends which narcotic traffickers and other
criminal enterprises make to avoid detection. The computer
would also be more objective and take away some of the concern of racial profiling. The computer would look at characteristics of criminal activity, not race or ethnic backgrounds.

Obviously to develop this program there are quite a few
hurdles to jump. Some hurdles found up to this point include

"right to privacy" or government access to private companies' records, the government acting as "big brother." The freight industry also has concerns about sharing shipment records between competing companies that might also be shared by law enforcement. Most companies have shown an interest in the program due to their belief that they have an obligation to run a clean company, be good responsible corporate citizens, and to keep criminal enterprises from using the industry to conduct criminal activity. Another and probably the bigger of the problems is financial side of the IT needs for computer scanning. What we have encountered when attempting to develop this program is that the IT personnel are extremely busy developing projects that enable the company to be more efficient and profitable. The other part is determining who would have the actual work assignment to review the information generated by the computer system and make the referral to the security department unless it could be built with an alert notification and send the qualifying suspicious shipments information directly to them. Normally, corporate security managers/investigators have worked with us, but sometimes, due to the relatively small number of these positions and the fact that they have to cover large areas of the country, they are not always immediately available.

Upon working with the freight industry while conducting freight interdiction operations, I have rarely found another industry more willing to work with law enforcement to keep the industry free of criminal activity. The employees we have contacted are extremely proud when they have assisted us in identifying shipments in which seizures have been made. I feel that the access to billing records could be overcome by developing tight and proper protocols for how and by whom this information is received and developed. The issue of developing the actual program with the technology people would possibly take funding from a grant to fund overtime for IT to work on this project outside normal responsibilities. It is currently anticipated very little if any funding would be needed for any other resources. The ability to receive this information upon computer scanning for suspicious shipments possibly could be overcome by law enforcement showing a commitment to the freight industry and gaining the trust of corporate to receive this information more directly (Matis 2006).

This proposal, although it was never acted upon, shows some thought into how the government and the industry could work together for a common goal without one having to acquiesce to the other. This program has validity even though several factors would have to be worked out. The main fact is that by using the known contraband profiles we have discussed in this book, many of the illicit shipments placed into the commercial systems could be identified and interdicted. Because no task force currently operating is using this information and informational sources, a high percentage of these shipments are not identified. When I worked in the industry and we identified one of these shipments, we would go back into the records using shipper and consignee information and usually we would find numerous shipments tied to the same sources which had traveled through the system to final delivery without being interdicted. Using these profiles allows investigators to work smarter and more efficiently than using a dog handler to scan millions of pounds of freight.

The DEA could easily setup a program like this that would not take a lot from what they do now and probably would provide significant return. DEA would be the agency that has the jurisdiction and capability of covering the shipments off the border and the first break points. This Bordernet proposal, drawn up by a city police detective working in a drug interdiction task force, is a good starting point. Personnel assigned to a unit like this would need to be educated on the workings of the industry and to build the public/private partnership with the involved companies but it is all very easily accomplished. Government agencies and agents currently do not use the resources available to them in most companies. The majority of security managers for medium to large transportation groups are former law enforcement personnel. They understand the rules of engagement on both sides of the fence and are more than happy to assist when wrongdoing is involved. Just recently, an NICB agent referred a federal law enforcement officer to me. The officer was doing a drug investigation that involved commercial vehicle shipments, and he needed information on how to locate certain information for his investigation. He provided a quick overview of his situation, and I was able to refer him to several sources that could help him find the information he needed. I did not need to know any secret information or be clued into any law enforcement sensitive data in order to guide him to sources where he could obtain the company and insurance information he was seeking. Why work harder than you have to? If a trusted resource is available, reach out and use it.

Over the years, members of the SWTSC companies have had issues with different federal agencies and operations or the checkpoints they operate which involve the transportation industry. Many times the decisions federal agencies make or the actions they take suggest that their agents have no idea how the different parts of the industry work. If they had that fundamental understanding, they could avoid taking actions that were not in the best interest of the involved company or its inspection or investigation. Many times by reaching out to a company security or operations manager, their questions could easily be answered and the issue resolved without detaining drivers or impeding freight operations. Many times, just by having a basic understanding of the modes of transportation operation, a proper investigative decision could be made. This is currently the exception and not the rule. Most companies want very much to cooperate and to operate in a lawful manner. Reach out to your public/private partnership groups like the councils and associations and make those contacts and build your resources. It helps everyone in the long run.

In the normal course of my daily activity, I receive bulletins involving the recovery of stolen cargo. One was in Dallas,

Texas, and the other in Kansas City, Missouri. The reason I mention these circumstances here is because both circumstances involved not only law enforcement personnel, but also insurance investigators and private investigators all working and sharing information with one another. Both operations recovered hundreds of thousands of dollars of goods. The point is that it takes everyone working together. I am proud of the networking we have put together with the councils and law enforcement and I see success from these actions almost every week. In the aforementioned Dallas recovery, every loss was reported through the council and several of the clues which lead to the recovery came from information passed between many different council members. This is what it is all about and is how it should work. As we move forward, we need to keep pushing the sharing of information and working together. Many law enforcement agencies and industry participants still need to hop aboard. This public/private partnership works and pays huge dividends.

Lobby for Formation of Cargo Theft Task Forces

As mentioned above, one of the recommendations of this book is to work toward establishing cargo theft task forces in locations which have been identified as having a large amount of cargo theft activity. Since the inception of the SWTSC in 1999, there have been two efforts to form a task force for this purpose in Texas. Both times the efforts were thwarted. During the first effort, many years ago, the FBI in Dallas, Texas, was willing to sponsor the task force and provide some funding for overtime and equipment, but the local law enforcement agencies would not provide the investigators needed. Many of the departments really did not understand the need. Several jurisdictions in the DFW Metroplex would really benefit from an organized group for this purpose, but their chiefs outsmarted themselves by turning down the assistance the group would have brought their investigators along with the extra funding. Assigning someone to a task force does not remove them from your department, they can still be assigned offenses, still be under the departmental control, but they now have access to assistance from the other task force members and the extra funding.

In 2010, another effort to put together a cargo theft task force for Texas was made. The effort was led by a former Irving, Texas, police chief and a member of the North Texas Crime Commission's Board of Directors. They put together a plan with the mission and organization and were able to take the information all the way to the governor's office. They made quite a bit of headway with legislators and garnered the backing of the National Insurance Crime Bureau, the SWTSC and others before their efforts fell short and they were unable to obtain funding. Their effort was appreciated by the industry and related associations and has led to other venues which may be open to getting cargo crime added to the responsibilities of current auto theft and auto burglary task forces that exist around the state.

Even though several of our efforts have been rejected, we keep trying to bring awareness to the people who need to know so that cargo theft prevention and investigation can be given consideration in law enforcement efforts beyond the hard work of each single jurisdiction. In Texas, we know that the majority of the cargo crime is in the Dallas/Fort Worth Metroplex and the Houston areas. If a task force were to be put in place, because of the miles between those areas, one task force would not be able to cover both areas easily. It would have to be organized like the California Highway Patrol Cargo Theft Interdiction program where they have different divisional assignment locations for the border, southern and northern areas, and use multi-agencies to fill their investigative detective slots. The mission of their investigations includes tractor and trailer theft, stolen property investigations (large quantities, multiple cases), theft of cargo stolen from warehouses, trailers and trains, and assisting allied agencies in like investigations. This set-up would work well in Texas. If not, we need to seek the assistance of the Auto Burglary Theft Prevention Authority (ABTPA) statewide task forces or at the least get the investigative agents of the Houston Area District of the Texas Department of Public Safety to add cargo theft as a priority, as was done in Dallas. The ABTPA route would take a dedicated funding source or a fee which could be assessed to provide dollars to the current ABTPA Task Forces so they could allocate manpower and time toward cargo along with their other duties. This funding source and idea is currently being studied. It is a proven fact that in areas where a cargo theft task force is in place law enforcement has much greater success in arrests and recovery.

The main thing for the industry is to keep looking at any and all remedies to support the creation of law enforcement task forces to engage in the investigation of this hard to pursue criminal activity.

The other states identified as having a problem with cargo theft include California, Georgia, New Jersey, and Illinois, and they have task forces. Florida, which is also identified as a problem area, just lost the TOMCATS, but still has some state police groups assigned to follow up cargo theft responsibility. The main focus continues to be in Texas and we will continue to work toward more resolutions for cargo theft investigation for our industry.

As far as cargo crime programs and cargo task forces go, what has been done in the past is the future. We must keep building the current industry council's membership and reach. These organizations have had a powerful impact and filled a large void where in the past there was nothing. The Southwest Transportation Security Council has more members and a far wider reach today to fill many needs, but there is much more we can do. To work at creating task forces or meeting any goal of the transportation security industry, there must be an organization and communication backbone from which to work. The system of communication that exists today because of the councils is unprecedented for this industry but is still a work in progress. Considering where the SWTSC started and where it is today, the progress is pretty amazing. The fact is that it has been involved in many success stories for both the police and the industry and that as a group it provides many services to its members and beyond. Those services include the BOLO/Alerts, law enforcement contacts, employment and job announcement services, and an industry and law enforcement assistance network that has connected the dots for many people, companies, and agencies around the country and into Canada and Mexico. We will continue to grow our council and assist other councils with formation and membership. The strength and reach of our council grows with the groups who network with us. The coming formation of the Virginia Carolina Cargo Security Council will really assist with the east coast port authorities and growing the law enforcement reach on Interstate 85 and 95 through those areas. We have seen increased cargo theft activity in Charleston, SC, in the past year so the forming of the VCCSC is good timing. This council will be a force multiplier for all of the current councils and is a welcome addition to the information share, networking, and vendor resources and solutions.

Finally, the job of organizing the transportation security industry is never done. Adding new councils or members is a welcome addition to the current arrangement and keeps the network growing and moving forward.

USING BEST PRACTICES

Chapter 8

Epilogue

Early in this book, I noted the wish of cargo security professionals to be able to quantify cargo theft. We looked at the Uniform Crime Reporting (UCR) definition of cargo theft and saw very convoluted reporting guidelines. We also learned as we traveled through this book that states that want to report crimes through the UCR system must have their own cargo theft statutes in place. Very few states currently have such statutes.

That restriction causes many cargo theft crimes to fall through the cracks and into other UCR index categories that are more easily identified by law enforcement reporting units. I do not believe the UCR system will ever resolve the issue. One reason is that it does not look at the UCR system from both the police and private sides.

We talked about the many modes of transportation and their practices. Private companies, especially consolidators such as LTL trucking firms, never report all of their losses to the police. They may report major losses with traceable serial numbers, but most pilferages and thefts of nonserialized products are handled through contractual agreements and internal claims and security investigations processes. A company investigation may or may not identify a suspect. A root-cause investigation may often identify weaknesses in

On one occasion, I suspected a driver working city deliveries and pick-ups from a south Texas terminal of several terminal thefts and was the focus of our investigation. We set up a sting by placing unmanifested freight on his delivery route and we planned to conduct surveillance. The freight (very expensive home hardware) was placed on his unit. The value of the freight made theft a felony offense according to the Texas Penal Code. I hired a private investigator to assist with the surveillance and placed a radio frequency beacon in the freight so that I could track the bait during the operation. We had a delivery manifest for the day so we know the driver's schedule for deliveries.

He left the terminal and went about making deliveries. After the third delivery, he drove south, off his expected route. We followed and confirmed via the beacon that the freight was on board his vehicle. The driver drove about 12 miles off route to a downtown area. He drove through alleys and small streets, making following him somewhat difficult. He stopped at a used clothing location that was not on his route or manifest and unloaded a shipment. After he left, I found that the beacon no longer emitted signals from his delivery unit. I returned to the used clothing store and I found that my RF beacon was chirping like a happy bird.

The private investigator and I entered the location and saw the suspected shipment. We recovered the shipment and interviewed women at the location who told us that the driver left the shipment and said he would return to pick it up later. We returned to the terminal and called the suspected driver to the terminal. Of course by then, he knew about the problem. He was interviewed. In a written statement, he admitted taking the property and not following company rules pertaining to unmanifested freight found on his unit.

I called the police and made a theft report. The case was assigned to an investigator many days later. He related that I should have involved the police in the surveillance. Because I did not do that, I would have to take the case directly to the district attorney. The district attorney, in turn, said that the police had to file the case. Obviously, I was stuck in the middle of law enforcement agencies that did not want to do their jobs.

At this point, the prosecution attempt was abandoned. The employee had resigned during his interview. About 18 months later, I learned that another LTL carrier had hired the suspected employee and now was also having theft issues. If he had been prosecuted, he probably would not have been hired by the next company. Because companies are restricted legally from passing on information about former employees, we see much of this kind of turnover in the industry. Remember, the best predictor of future behavior is past behavior and that analogy seldom fails, no matter the time span.

the process that allow exceptions to happen and operational adjustments will be made

If a suspect is identified, security investigators will determine whether the offense is reportable because the company has supportable evidence, in which case the police will be engaged. If not, an employee suspect may be terminated or allowed to resign and all parties move forward. When I worked for an LTL, I investigated several such thefts. Depending on the evidence or circumstance, we may have given the investigation information to the police who would file a case, usually if the case was a felony and good evidence existed to support the prosecution.

If the facts and the value of a theft do not meet certain thresholds, they are handled internally and never reported. That is a reality of the shipping business and will probably never change. Smaller thefts and exceptions will always be dealt with in the most efficient way and reporting the information to the police is not always necessary or practical. Many times it is easier to solve the problem and move on.

Learning from Reality

We as an industry must be the force that causes law enforcement officers to engage regarding cargo theft and other offenses. I believe that one of the best approaches is through local auto theft units and detectives assigned to commercial vehicle theft investigation and also though the International Association of Auto Theft Investigators (IAATI) and its regional affiliates. These parties understand the connection of auto theft and cargo theft and many of them are already actively working such cases. Through my association with LoJack Corporation, I have already provided organizations and regional affiliates with cargo theft training and I attend most of their conferences to network with detectives around the country. Pat Clancy, LoJack's director of law enforcement, has been a great advocate for a partnership of IAATI members and the cargo industry. Pat has encouraged his law enforcement liaisons around the country to assist with cargo thefts and recoveries.

As I have said throughout this book, the freight industry must protect itself. The police will assist, but the industry must forge networks and foster contacts or it will be left calling 911 like other crime victims. We do not want that. We want relationships with law enforcement departments, agencies, and officers who will attend training conferences, pay attention to our criminal issues, and help when needed. Building those relationships is imperative. If everyone in the industry builds networks and shares information, the force multipliers are in action.

The SWTSC and other councils support the law enforcement groups that work our industry cases in every way possible. I have seen the positive sides of such relationships and also felt the isolation of not having a direct connection when needed. If everyone who works in the industry adds one police investigator to the distribution lists of the councils that provide BOLO alerts and participates in SC-ISAC or CargoNet efforts, they are building something that is much bigger than any single entity. I have a very full Rolodex and over 500 contacts in my cell phone. They are not enough. I will never refuse to assist anyone who needs a law enforcement connection. I may not be able to do it in every case but I will make the effort.

Most people who contact me are assisted quickly. A contact not entered in my cell phone might be on the SWTSC distribution list or among my computer contacts. If law enforcement needs a contact in the industry, the SWTSC can usually provide one. The goal of every good company investigator should be to build a personal network that in turns builds the industry's network and reach

A glossary of freight and transportation security words and acronyms is included at the end of this book to help explain the language of the industry and related security terms.

Future work is simple: keep doing what we have been doing by supporting entities that advocate and promote information sharing and public–private partnerships. Understand your industry and the criminal elements that attack and exploit it. Awareness, education, and communication are the answers to most problems, even cargo theft. With a full knowledge of the risks and threats, it is easy to set in place a plan to prevent incidents and protect an operation. Cargo industry operations have many similarities and also differences. Every company has unique needs and requirements to make its operations secure. This book covered the many risks, discussed the collected and analyzed cargo theft data, and explained criminal methods of operation and the threats facing each mode of transportation. Although the industry is complex and moving freight is a far more complicated operation than it appears, the vital information in this book will help you make the best decisions in operations and security planning for your employer.

Dialing 911 should not be your recovery plan and the government's Global Supply Chain National Strategy is not your security plan! You can do much better!

Appendix: Southwest Transportation Security Council Freight Term Glossary

Abloy: High-strength transportation lock.

Absolute minimum: Minimum charge below which a carrier will not discount.

Access control: Control of persons, vehicles, and materials by implementation of security measures for a protected area.

Accessorial service: Service rendered by a carrier in addition to regular service typically for a fee.

Adjudicate: Settle or determine a matter finally through the course of judicial authority. In criminal justice usage, the term is used with reference to a judgment of acquittal or conviction.

AG IMP: Agricultural implement.

AGPS: Assisted global positioning satellite.

Air bag: Bag designed to secure and block freight loaded in trailers by using air pressure.

Alarm system: Combination of sensors, controls, and annunciators arranged to detect and report an intrusion or other emergency.

All short: Exception indicating that there is no freight to match a shipping document.

AMC: Account management center.

Arbitrary (Arb): Charge added to certain delivery points or for various activities to cover additional expense.

Arrival notice: Written or verbal notice to consignee that a shipment has arrived.

Asset protection: Shielding from danger or harm the money, receivables, information, resources, rights, property, and other valuables of an owner.

A sheet: Reference in multiple load manifests for loads going to separate destinations including A, B, and sometimes C sheets and loads.

Astray freight: Freight separated from its billing documents.

Attempt: Act done with intent to commit a crime but falling short of its actual commission; a form of conduct coupled with intent that tends to effect the commission of a crime.

Audit: Examination of procedures and practices for the purposes of identifying and correcting unwanted conditions.

Axle weight: Amount of weight bearing on one axle.

Back haul: Traffic moving in direction of light flow when a carrier's traffic in a given lane is heavier in one direction than the other or moving a load back to original origin.

Background screening: Inquiry into history and behaviors of an individual under consideration for employment.

Banding machine: Dock machine used to install straps.

Barrel wheeler or truck: Dolly hand truck built to move drums and barrels.

BBL: Barrel.

BDL: Bundle.

Best practices: Elements found to be successful such as policy and planning as guides, work rules and procedures as directives, risk assessment, crime opportunity reduction, and training of employees.

Bill of lading: Legal contract between shipper and carrier to move goods; may serve as shipper's receipt.

Bill to: Designation for billing to a responsible party.

Blind side: Nondriver side of vehicle.

Blocking: Supports to stabilize shipment loaded in trailer.

Bob tail: Tractor operating without trailer.

Bogie: Two-axle assembly or tandem axle.

BOL or B/L: Bill of lading.

BOLO: Be on the lookout (theft alert).

Bonded warehouse: Location authorized by government, under bond, for observance of revenue laws.

Bottom freight: Heavy freight or floor freight that cannot be stacked or loaded on other freight.

Box: Trailer or semitrailer.

Bracing: Same as blocking.

Break bulk: Point where freight is exchanged or consolidated for continued movement to final delivery destinations.

Broker: Person or company that arranges truck transportation of cargo belonging to others, using for-hire carriers to provide transportation.

Bulk freight: Nonpackaged or containerized freight.

Bulkhead: Wall built in trailer to stabilize freight in-transit.

Burden of proof: Burden on prosecuting authority to prove guilt of a defendant beyond a reasonable doubt.

BX: Box.

Cab: Driver's compartment of truck or tractor.

Cable seal: Heavy steel cable used to secure closed trailer doors.

Cab-over: Driver compartment substantially over the engine compartment.

Canine security: Use of dogs in security for guarding property, protecting people, and detecting drugs and explosives.

Capacity load: Trailer loaded to either legal weight or where no additional piece can be added.

Cargo Intelligence Process: Continuous cycle of information collection, evaluation, analysis, collation, reporting, and dissemination directed toward converting raw information into material useful for cargo theft prevention and awareness.

Cargo liability insurance: Motor truck cargo insurance coverage purchased to protect truck drivers and carriers from liability for transported cargo that belongs to shippers or clients.

Cargo security: Multilayered, multimode approach to secure cargo in transit in the supply chain.

Cart: Four-wheeled dock dolly for moving freight.

Cartage: Hauling between locations in same area or P&D of freight within a commercial zone acting as agent for shipper or over the road (OTR) carrier.

Cash collect: Order to collect cash at point of delivery.

CBP: Customs and border protection.

CDL: Commercial driver's license.

Check stand: Dock desk at loading door.

Checkstop: Regular scheduled stop at customer location.

CHEM: Chemicals.

Chock: Wedge used to block trailer tires or to block freight in a trailer.

CHP CTIP: California Highway Patrol Cargo Theft Interdiction Program.

Claim: Demand made for payment from carrier for loss or damage.

Claim tracer: Claim status request.

Claimant: Filer of a claim.

Class rate: Transportation rate established for a group of commodities.

Classification of freight: Category assigned an article of freight according to the National Motor Freight Classification (NMFC).

Clean BOL: Signed delivery receipt with no exceptions.

COBZ: Company business shipment.

COD: Collect on delivery.

COLL: Collect.

Collect shipment: Shipment paid for upon delivery to consignee.

Combination: Truck or tractor coupled to one or more trailers.

Commodity: Cargo articles, goods, or merchandise.

Commodity rate: Special rate for specific goods.

Commodity tariff: Tariff of commodity rates.

Common carrier: Transportation company that offers service to the general public.

Concealed damage: Damage not apparent and subsequently not noted on delivery receipt.

Concealed loss: Loss that is not apparent and subsequently not noted on delivery receipt.

Connecting carrier: Carrier that originates or completes shipment but does not handle entire shipment.

CONS: Consignee.

Consequential damages: Special damages related to additional cost of loss or damages based on loss of profit or advertising promises.

Consign: Send goods.

Consignee: Receiver of goods.

Consignor: Shipper.

Constant surveillance service: System by which a shipment is signed for and confirmed at each point of consolidation.

Contingent cargo insurance: Coverage that takes over a claim if primary cargo liability policy fails to provide coverage or is not adequate to cover the entire loss. A contingent cargo liability policy pays any remaining losses subject to conditions of the policy.

Contract carrier: Company that engages in for-hire transportation of property under contracts with one or more shippers.

Contract rate: Rate agreed upon by shipper and carrier.

Contract security: Protective services provided by a company specializing in such services to another company on a paid contractual basis.

Control panel: Centrally located assembly containing power supplies, relays, amplifiers, and other equipment needed to receive, interpret, and supervise alarm signals from a protected area; device that arms, disarms, and supervises an alarm system.

Controlled access area: Clearly demarcated area, access to which is controlled, that affords isolation of materials or persons within it.

Controlled lighting: Exterior lighting that directs illumination on a particular area.

Conventional cab: Tractor with engine in front of cab.

Copy bill: Copy of original movement document used when the original is lost.

Corrective action: Action to eliminate the cause of a detected operational or security flaw.

COSO: Copy of shipment order.

Covert cargo tracking: AGPS tracking technology. An AGPS device is placed in cargo to produce reports on location of the load.

Cross dock: Transfer of freight from one trailer to another.

CSS: Constant surveillance service.

CTN: Carton.

C-TPAT: Customs Trade Partnership against Terrorism; voluntary government–industry program to create and secure an efficient supply chain for importers.

Cube: Cubic capacity of a trailer, usually by percentage.

Cubic capacity: Carrying capacity of trailer measured in cubic feet.

CWT: Hundred weight.

Dead axle: Nonpowered rear axle on tandem truck or tractor.

Deadhead: Trailer moving empty or uncharged shipment.

Delivery set: Freight bill delivery set.

DELY or DLVY or DELV: Deliver.

Demurrage: Detention charge for freight vehicle or container beyond stipulated time and payment.

Density: Weight of an article per cubic foot.

DEST: Destination.

Detention: Charge made for held vehicle or for consignee loading.

DHS: Department of Homeland Security.

Diagraph marker: Dock tool used for marking metal.

Direct loss: Dollar measure of costs associated with loss of money, negotiable instruments, property, information, and personnel; a loss that is a direct consequence of a particular peril.

Dispatching: Scheduling of line-haul or P&D routing.

Diversion: Change in routing that will require a new freight bill (reconsignment).

Dock: Area where trucks load, unload, or consolidate.

Dock drop: Delivery of freight to origin dock by a shipper or its representative.

Dock pick-up: Consignee picks up shipment at destination dock.

Dock plate: Metal plate used to bridge space between dock and trailer.

Dolly: Single-axle device used to couple two trailers together; non-motorized two-wheel hand truck.

Domicile: Driver's home base location.

DOT: Department of Transportation.

D/R: Delivery receipt.

Drayage: Charge for hauling freight, usually by local cartage agents.

Drive axle: Power axle powered by drive shaft.

Driver collect: Driver collect fee upon delivery.

Driver sales representative: Driver who interacts directly with customers.

Drums: Barrels.

DSR: Driver sales representative.

Dual: Pair of tires mounted together.

Dub: Twenty-eight-foot trailer designed to be pulled two or three at a time.

Dunnage: Wood, cardboard, foam rubber, air bags, or other items used to block or cushion freight.

EDI: Electronic data exchange.

ELEC: Electric or electronic.

Electronic countermeasure: Defensive technique designed to detect, prevent, or expose the use of electronic communication surveillance devices.

EOL: End of line.

Equip: Equipment.

ERCTA: Eastern Region Cargo Theft Association; an industry regional cargo security council in the northeast region of the United States.

Escort: Security convoy providing physical presence to protect high-value shipments.

Exception: Shortage, overage, or damage to a shipment.

Exclusive use: Use of one trailer by one customer for a fee.

EXPD: Expedite.

Expedite: Form for moving astray freight to its proper destination.

Extension: Long forklift blades

FAC: Freight assembly center.

FAK: Freight of all kinds.

FAST: Free and secure trade.

FB: Freight bill.

Fence: Person who receives or buys and then sells stolen goods, usually as a business.

Fictitious Pick-up: Theft of identity of individual or company and using Identity to pose as contract transportation carrier and bid for loads on Internet load boards; load is picked up and never delivered.

Fifth wheel: Device on back of tractor that hooks to king pin of trailer.

Fingerman: Person who provides information on a truck marked for hijacking by supplying a description of the truck, cargo, plate number, road route, departure time, schedule of stops, arrival time, and similar details of interest to cargo thieves.

FLF: Forklift.

Forced entry: Entry accomplished by the use of force on physical components of premises or vehicle using tools or muscle power.

Forklift: Vehicle used on a dock to lift and move freight.

FRCE: Forced bill; delivery of over freight.

Free Astray: MOVR Pro for moving astray freight free of charge to correct destination.

Free on Board (FOB): Ownership of goods passes to consignee after shipment is loaded.

Free time: Period before stored freight charges are applied.

Freight bill: Transportation company invoice showing Information about movements and charges.

Freight forwarder: Company that owns no means of transportation and obtains space for freight transportation from providers. It then sells space to customers.

Freight of all kinds (FAK): Procedure to classify all freight the same for a single rating.

FRT: Freight.

FTGS: Fittings.

FTL: Full truckload; trucking company that handles high-volume shipping and utilizes one trailer to transport freight for one shipper.

Full visible capacity: Trailer loaded to point where no additional piece can be added.

Gateway: Point at which freight leaves one country and enters another.

Gaylord container: Pallet size container for movement of liquid shipments.

GBL: Government bill of lading.

GCBZ: General claims business.

Geo fence: Virtual fence that defines a geographical area; can be used to generate an alert when an asset enters or exits an area.

Glad hand: Coupling on the front of a trailer to which the air brake hoses are connected to couple the tractor and trailer brake systems.

Glad hand lock: Lock that prevents air brake hoses from being connected to a trailer.

Global positioning satellite (GPS): System that provides location fixes through a mapping interface from a set of geostationary satellites orbiting above the earth.

GPS: Global positioning satellite.

Gross negligence: Intentional failure to perform a duty in reckless disregard of consequences that may affect the life or property of another; lack of ordinary or even slight care.

Gross weight: Weight of contents, packing, and equipment.

HAZ MAT: Hazardous material.

HDWE: Hardware.

Header: Shipment loaded in front or nose of a trailer.

HHG: Household goods.

High and tight: Using full cube of a trailer.

Hijacking: Taking control of a vehicle by threat, use of force, or intimidation.

HM: Hazardous material; substance or material determined by US Secretary of Transportation to be capable of posing significant risk.

Homeland security: Federal government effort in coordination with state and local governments and the private sector to develop, coordinate, fund, and implement programs and policies necessary to detect, prepare for, prevent, protect against, respond to, and recover from terrorist or other attacks within the United States.

Hostler: Employee who moves trailers to and from a dock in a yard.

Hostling tractor: Tractor used to move trailers to and from a dock and around a yard.

Hotline: Dedicated telephone line used exclusively for receiving security tips; part of a reward system.

Hot shipment: Shipment that requires special attention or priority delivery.

Hot wire: Starting a vehicle without using a key, for example, using an electrical jumper wire.

Hybrid locking system: Locking system that derives its security from two or more different technologies operated by the same key in one device.

I&E: Income and expense.

I/S: Iron and/or steel.

In bond: Goods on which duties or taxes become due and are placed in a government-bonded warehouse.

Indemnification: Compensating insured individuals for their losses; restoring the victim of a loss to the position that existed before the loss occurred.

Indemnity: Insurance contract to reimburse an individual or organization for possible losses of a specific type.

Indirect loss: Loss that results from a peril or theft beyond the direct loss of a product. Examples are remanufacturing costs, replacement costs, and losses incurred when product is unavailable.

Information security: Protection of information against unauthorized disclosure, transfer, modification, and destruction.

In-house security: Protective services provided company employees.

Inside delivery: Delivery that requires moving freight to positions further than adjacent to a trailer. for example, to a mall or downtown building. Usually an additional charge is added for this service.

Integrity seal: Seal that provides clear evidence that it has been tampered with or illegitimately opened.

Interface: Mapping and controlling screen for AGPS covert cargo-tracking technology.

Interline: Transfer of freight between companies.

Intermodal: Involving more than one mode of transportation.

Interstate: Between states.

Intrastate: Within one state.

Invoice attachment: Document needed for payment, usually a delivery receipt (DR).

ISO: Insurance services office.

Jammer: Radio frequency or audio frequency oscillator that interferes with the operation of an electronic audio surveillance system.

Jamming: Deliberate introduction of radio frequencies, electrical signals, or physical objects that are not normal to the operation of a circuit or device.

Johnson bar: Large crowbar used on freight docks.

KD: Knocked down.

KDF: Knocked down flat.

Key control system: Special cabinet, tray, or other enclosure for storing keys in an organized system and protecting them from unauthorized removal.

King pin: Large steel pin under the front of a trailer designed to mate with fifth wheel on a tractor for towing.

King pin lock: Lock designed to attach to king pin of trailer that prevents the unit from being connected to the fifth wheel of a tractor.

Known damage: Damage discovered before or at time of delivery and notated on a delivery receipt as an exception.

Known loss: Loss discovered before or at time of delivery and notated on a delivery receipt as an exception.

Landing gear: Support legs at front of a trailer that hold it up when It is detached from the tractor.

Lane: Movement between origin and destination service points.

Layered security: Physical security approach that requires a criminal to penetrate or overcome a series of security layers before reaching a target.

LH: Line haul.

Lift jab: Boom of portable crane that lifts objects with a chain or cable.

Lift truck: Forklift or tow motor.

Line haul: Movement of freight from one service center to another (unlike city P&D).

Live axle: Axle powered by engine via drive shaft.

Load bar: Portable adjustable metal bar used to stabilize freight loads in a trailer.

Load factor: Weight in pounds loaded onto a trailer; the greater the load factor, the lower the cost.

Load manifest: Bill pack acting as summary of trailer contents (TCON).

Log book: Book containing daily records of hours and routes of line-haul drivers required by U.S. DOT.

LPG: Liquid petroleum gas.

LSE: Loose.

LTD QTY: Limited quantity.

LTL: Less than truckload; type of trucking company that specializes in small-volume hauling by consolidating multiple clients' freight loads.

LTL rate: Rate applicable to LTL shipments.

Manifest: Document containing trailer content information used for control purposes during loading and unloading.

Marine cargo insurance: Protection of cargo shipped internationally, usually by sea or air, to protect the owner or carrier in the event of loss due to exposure to weather, jettison, theft, mishandling, and damages arising from loading and unloading. Other special circumstances such as equipment breakdowns and delays that expose perishable items can also be insured.

Mark: Slang term for a shipment.

Marking or mark: Letters, numbers, or characters placed on a container for identification.

Master bill: Summary bill for a shipper; not a freight control document.

Meet and turn: Over-the-road (OTR) meeting point where drivers exchange loads and return to their domiciles.

Mid-South Cargo Security Council: Industry cargo security council based in Memphis, TN.

Mid-West Cargo Security Council: Regional industry security council based in Chicago, IL.

Mid-West Cargo Task Force: Illinois State Police cargo task force.

Mileage rate: Rate based on mileage instead of commodity.

Mileage tariff: Tariff containing mileage rates.

Minimum charge: Lowest charge for which a shipment can be handled.

Mix: Combination of freight weights used to max out weight and cube of a trailer.

Mode: Basic type of freight transportation.

Monitoring by exception: Electronic alert system that annunciates only when an undesirable act takes place.

Motion detection: Detection of an intruder by monitoring movement in a protected area.

Motion detection alarm: System that monitors motion in an area under surveillance.

Motor truck cargo insurance: Insurance that protects an owner or carrier against certain types of perils like theft, damage during transit, and other occurrences that cause loss depending on the type of cargo shipped. Most products that are shipped over the road can and should have specific coverage under a motor truck cargo insurance policy.

MOVR: Bill used to move astray overfreight to its original PRO destination; matched over freight.

MSCSC: Mid-South Cargo Security Council.

MSDS: Material safety data sheet.

MSTR: Master bill.

MTL: Material.

NAE: National account executive.

Narcotic: Drug that dulls a person's senses and produces a sense of well-being.

Negligence: Doing something a reasonably prudent person would not do, or the failure to do something a reasonably prudent person would do in similar circumstances.

Negligent hiring: Failure to use reasonable selection in the employee hiring process, resulting in harm caused to others.

Nested: Freight packed within other freight.

Net weight: Weight of trailer contents excluding the trailer.

NICB: National Insurance Crime Bureau; organization that provides agents to assist in investigating insurance fraud and cargo crime.

NMFC: National motor freight classification. Motor carrier publication containing regulations, commodity descriptions. and classifications for most shippable commodities.

NOI: Not otherwise indexed (in NMFC).

Nose: Front of trailer.

Noseload: Same as header.

Noted damage: Freight damage discovered and noted prior to or during delivery.

NVOCC: Non-vessel operating common carrier.

O/O: Owner operator.

Open Cargo Insurance: Insurance for carriers and owners that covers large volumes of cargo. Several types of policies provide broad coverage for many areas of truck and marine operations. One of the most common is an open perils or open cargo policy. Any party with a vested interest can insure a certain agreed value, a specified period of time, or both. These policies are broad and do not usually list the details of the specific transaction such as the name of a ship, destination, or other details because they cover an agreed value or losses during a specific time.

Open-top trailer: Trailer with removable tarpaulin cover; rag top.

Operating ratio: Relationship of total expenses to total revenues.

Operational audit: Examination of operations of an enterprise to ensure that the activities performed are consistent with expressed policy and best practices.

Operational intelligence: Intelligence acquired for planning and executing operations consistent with a company strategy.

O/R: Operating ratio.

OREP: Over report; report covering delivery of pieces in excess of billed piece count.

Organized crime: Organized criminal activity of persons who engage in crime as a primary source of income and cooperate and coordinate illegal activities including cargo thefts.

ORM: Other regulated materials.

OS&D: Over, short, and damaged; exception between freight on hand and freight on bill.

OTR: Over the road.

Over freight: Freight separated from movement control document or more freight than noted on shipment document.

Over-the-counter (OTC) Drugs: Drugs that may be purchased without prescription.

OWB: Over without bill.

Owner-operator: Self-employed independent driver who operates an owned or leased truck; not a company driver.

Pallet: Wooden platform on which freight is stacked during shipping.

Pallet jack: Hand-operated lift tool used on dock.

Palletized: Stacked on pallets.

Part Lot PRO: Umbrella PRO number used to cover all parts of a split shipment moved in more than one trailer.

Payload: Net weight of cargo.

PCS: Pieces.

P&D: Pick-up and delivery.

Peddle freight: Shipment delivered from service center to far-reaching points of service area.

Peddle run: Pick-up or delivery made outside normal service center coverage area.

Perimeter barrier: Physical barrier around perimeter of a protected area to prevent or delay entry.

Perishable freight: Freight that can deteriorate or decay if not stored properly or delivered on time.

Physical security: Security involving physical measures designed to prevent unauthorized access to equipment, facilities, materials, and documents.

Pig: Trailer or container transported on a rail car.

Piggyback: Transportation of highway trailer on a flat rail car.

Pintle hook: Hook mounted on a trailer to connect with the eye of a dolly trailer.

PLT: Pallet.

Pool shipment: Shipper's consolidation of several shipments destined to different delivery points into a single shipment for a carrier.

Powered axle: Drive (powered) axle of a tractor.

PPD: Prepaid.

PPR: Paper.

Prepaid: Payment for shipping is made at origin or shipper is responsible.

Private search concept: Searches undertaken by private persons or companies are not subject to constitutional regulation.

PRO (tracking) number: Carrier control number that links all related freight movement documents to a shipment.

Proof of delivery (POD): Delivery receipt signed by consignee.

Property crime: Offenses against property such as burglary, larceny, motor vehicle, cargo, and other theft.

PSEG: Part segment (billing term).

PTLT: Part lot (billing term).

PTS: Parts.

PU: Pick-up.

Pull the pin: Release fifth wheel lock.

Pup: Twenty-eight foot trailer designed for multiple uses or to make city pick-ups and deliveries.

Pyramid: Palletized freight stacked in pyramid pattern.

Radiofrequency motion detection: Use of radiofrequency generating and receiving equipment to detect the presence of an intruder.

Rag top: Open-top trailer that may have tarpaulin cover.

Rail trailers: Trailer usually provided by railroad for loading on flat railcar.

Rate: Charge per hundred weight for transporting freight.

Reconsignment: Change in routing or destination for in-transit freight.

Recooper: Repair damaged cartons or containers.

Recovery plan: Documented collection of procedures and information maintained in readiness for use after a cargo theft incident.

Reefer: Refrigerated trailer.

Release value: Value specified by a shipper to establish carrier's minimum liability.

Residential delivery: Delivery to private residence; involves accessorial charge.

Restitution: Returning stolen money or property; may be done voluntarily or ordered by a court as part of a sentence or as a condition of probation.

Revenue PRO: PRO number or bill used to capture revenue.

Reverse sting: Law enforcement strategy in which undercover police pose as criminals and arrest persons who plan or engage in illegal activity.

RF: Radiofrequency.

RFID: Radiofrequency identification.

Root cause analysis: Technique used to identify circumstances that initiate an undesired activity or state.

Rug pole: Forklift attachment.

S/O: Shipping order.

SC-ISAC: Supply Chain-Information Sharing and Analysis Center.

Seal: Numbered aluminum or plastic strip fastened to a closed trailer door to verify door integrity during transit.

Security: Protection against hazards, threats, risks, and losses.

Security manager: Management-level employee with responsibility for the security of an organization or facility.

SED: Shipper's export declaration.

Semi: Trailer 48- to 53-feet-long equipped with rear wheels and landing gear.

SETSC: Southeast Transportation Security Council.

Shipper load and count: Indication that the contents of a trailer or pallet were loaded and counted by a shipper and the carrier did not participate in loading.

Shipper's interest insurance: Coverage needed when the value of a load exceeds the amount of insurance carried by the carrier slated to haul the shipment.

Shipping papers: Documents covering freight movements; the COSO usually is the only document that travels with a shipment.

Shore power: Land-based electric power supply for trucks. Eliminates the need for engine idling while parked; may include climate control within the truck cab and Internet and TV access.

Short or shortage: Number of pieces in a shipment fewer than number indicated on the freight bill.

Shrink wrap: Plastic wrap used to secure cartons on a pallet.

Shrinkage: Decrease in inventory or loss of volume, usually applied to a decrease by reason of employee pilferage.

SIC: Standard identification code.

Signature security service: Service designed to provide continuous responsibility for the custody of shipments in transit that requires written acknowledgement by each person handling the shipment at each stage (consolidation) from point of origin to destination.

Single shipment: Shipment weighing less than 500 pounds and picked up at customer's dock; subject to accessorial fee.

Skid: Wooden or plastic platform upon which freight is stacked; base has clearance for lift blades.

SL&C: Shipper load and count.

Slam hammer: Tool used by car thieves and cargo thieves to remove cylinders of ignition locks.

Sleeper: Tractor with sleeping compartment.

Sleeper run: No-layover line-haul with two drivers taking turns sleeping and driving.

Sliding fifth wheel: Adjustable fifth wheel used to obtain desired load distribution.

Smuggling: Illegal transport of contraband (drugs, people, unauthorized freight) usually via commercial vehicles and transit systems.

Southeast Transportation Security Council: Regional industry security council based in Atlanta.

Southwest Transportation Security Council (SWTSC): Regional industry security council based in Dallas.

Special damages: Damages in excess of the actual freight damage such as losses of profit and losses arising from promises of delivery for advertised products.

Spectrum analyzer: Electronic device that detects the presence of radiofrequency transmissions characteristic of covertly installed transmitters.

Split pick-up or delivery: Multiple location service subject to accessorial charge.

Spot a trailer: Park a trailer.

Spotter: Yard employee who parks trailers.

Staging: Assembling material and equipment in a particular place.

Stakeholder: Person or group that has an interest in the performance or success of an organization.

Stop In transit: Scheduled stop to load or deliver en route, usually involving an accessorial charge.

Straight truck: Truck with power unit and van body in one piece.

Stretch wrap: Shrink wrap.

Strip: Unload, count, and check a trailer.

Subpoena: Written order issued by a judicial officer requiring a specified person to appear as a witness in a case and/or produce written records to the court.

Supply chain: Set of linked resources and processes that begins with the acquisition of raw material and extends through the delivery of products or services to end users across the modes of transport; may include suppliers, vendors, manufacturing facilities, logistics providers, internal distribution centers, distributors, wholesalers, and other entities involved with movement of products to end users.

Surcharge: Additional charge, most commonly for fuel.

Surveillance: Covert observation of a location, activity, or person.

Suspect: Person considered by a criminal justice agency to have committed a criminal offense before he or she is arrested or charged.

SWTSC: Southwest Transportation Security Council.

SYN: Synthetic.

TAMCATS: Tennessee–Arkansas–Mississippi Cargo Auto Theft Task Force.

Tandem: Semitrailer, truck, or tractor with two rear axles to allow for carrying of larger payloads.

Tare weight: Weight of container and packing material; weight of truck exclusive of contents.

Tariff: Published list of transportation rates, charges, and rules.

Tarpaulin or tarp: Cover for open-top rig.

TCON: List of all PRO numbers in loaded trailer; trailer contents.

Team drivers: Two or more drivers who ride together and drive the same truck in shifts, essentially allowing the truck to remain in motion almost constantly. Primarily used for time-sensitive or high-value freight.

Technical security: Measures used to identify and prevent technical threats including electronic wiretapping, bugging, eavesdropping, signal intercepts, covert surveillance, and attacks on information technology and communications systems.

Theft: Group of offenses including larceny, burglary, extortion, fraud that share the intent of depriving an owner of property.

Third party billing: Billing to a party that neither the shipper nor the consignee.

Third party logistic provider (3PL): Entity that handles transportation and logistics for a shipper.

Through rate: Rate covering shipment from origin to destination as opposed to interline combo rates.

TL: Truckload.

TM: Traffic manager.

TMAN: Trailer manifest. Document used to check load during unloading; contains PRO numbers, pieces, weight, and destination standard identification code (SIC).

T/O: Transport operator.

TOFC: Trailer on flat car.

Top freight: Light or fragile freight that should be loaded on top of a cube.

Top-heavy freight: Freight that must be restrained to prevent falling or damage.

Trace: Determine shipment location.

Tracer: Request to carrier to locate a shipment.

Tracking GPS: Obtaining location report via global positioning satellite through a mapping interface.

Tractor: Power unit for pulling trailers.

Traffic manager: Controller of outbound and inbound freight movements at a location or for an entire company.

Trailer on flat car (TOFC): Transport of a highway trailer on a rail flat car; piggyback.

Trap trailer: Trailer used to store or stage freight, usually high-value freight, secured with locks and under supervisory control.

Trip lease: Hire of an owner operator to make a single trip.

Triple: Tractor pulling three trailers (pups).

Truckload: Quantity of freight that will fill a vehicle or weigh legal maximum.

TSA: Transportation Security Administration.

TWIC: Transportation worker identification card.

Unloading check sheet: Reverse of trailer manifest; exceptions and freight left on are noted.

Vendor audit: Examination of the records of transactions between a purchaser and a vendor to determine continued compliance to contract requirements and guidelines.

Vet: Legally examine; physically inspect; inquire, for example, during a security investigation or background check for potential employees or service providers.

Via: Line haul stop to load or deliver.

Virtual geo fence: See geo fence.

Voyage Insurance: Coverage to ensure that a cargo moves from its place of origin to its final destination. This type of policy has more specific details than an open-cargo policy because it applies to a trip from a specific origination to a specific destination. Because of the many types of potential delays, the length of the passage is not typically stated. After the cargo is delivered to the specified destination, the policy typically expires.

Vulnerability analysis: Method of identifying the weak points of a facility, entity, location, or transit route.

WT: Weight.

WVN: Woven

Warehouseman's liability: Less than full common carrier liability based on reasonable care while freight is in carrier's possession.

War-Lok: Transportation locking device.

White collar crime: Wide variety of typically nonviolent crimes that involve deception, corruption, and unauthorized use of company assets.

Yard goat or mule: Hostling tractor used to move trailers around terminal yards.

Zone: Section of alarmed, protected, or patrolled area.

Zone terminal location: Not fully staffed service center established in area of substantial business activity.

Bibliography

Cargo theft reporting improves says insurers' CargoNet. 2012. *Insurance Journal*.

Coughlin, J.J. 2011a. *SC-ISAC Cargo Theft Report*. Forney: SC-ISAC.

Coughlin, J.J. 2011b. *BOLO Theft Alert*. Dallas: Southwest Transportation Security Council.

Coughlin, J.J. 2010. *SC-ISAC Cargo Theft Report*. Forney: SC-ISAC.

Coughlin, J.J. and Lewis, S. 2010. *Best Supply Chain Security Practices*. Dallas: Southwest Transportation Security Council.

Coughlin, J.J. 2009a. *SC-ISAC Cargo Theft Report*. Forney: SC-ISAC.

Coughlin, J.J. 2009b. Cargo Theft Template. Dallas: Southwest Transportation Security Council.

Coughlin, J.J. 2001. Driver Warning Sheet.

Coughlin, J.J. No date. *Interdiction: Company Operation and Documentation*. Presentation. Dallas: Southwest Transportation Security Council.

Dallas Police Department. 2012. *Crime Report: Reporting Areas 4375 and 4376*.

Hawkins, M. 2011. *California Highway Patrol Cargo Theft Interdiction Program Cargo Theft Report*. Los Angeles: California Highway Patrol.

Hohenberger, S. 2012. *Cargo Theft Statute*. Proposed Legislation, Dallas: NICB.

Marsh USA. 2012. Global insurance market quarterly briefing: first quarter. *Insurance Journal*.

Matis, E. 2006. *Bordernet Proposal*. Dallas: Dallas–Fort Worth Drug Interdiction Task Force.

Texas, State of. 2010. *Texas Penal Code, Chapter 31: Theft*. Austin: State of Texas.

US Department of Justice. No date. Cargo Theft UCR Definition. Washington: USDOJ.

US Food & Drug Administration. 2012. *FDA's Response to Cargo Theft: Staff Manual Guide*, Vol. IV. Washington: US, Department of Health & Human Services.

Index

C

D

E